SOCIAL
WORK ISSUES:
STRESS, THE TEA PARTY,
ROE VERSUS WADE
AND EMPOWERMENT

SOCIAL WORK ISSUES:
STRESS, THE TEA PARTY, ROE VERSUS WADE AND EMPOWERMENT

FRANCIS BORBOH DUMBUYA

"Your story is our priority"

LitPrime Solutions
21250 Hawthorne Blvd
Suite 500, Torrance, CA 90503
www.litprime.com
Phone: 1-800-981-9893

Published by LitPrime Solutions   02/28/2023

ISBN: 979-8-88703-149-1(sc)
ISBN: 979-8-88703-150-7(hc)
ISBN: 979-8-88703-151-4(e)

Library of Congress Control Number: 2023900799

CONTENTS

CHAPTER ONE

CHAPTER TWO

CHAPTER THREE

CHAPTER FOUR

CHAPTER FIVE

CHAPTER ONE

Work-related stress is a growing problem in occupational organisations and this problem is affecting employees as well as organisations adversely in terms of human and economic costs. The changing nature of work and the diversity of the employees amongst other things have heightened the topic of work-related stress within professional groups. Various professional groups experience and perceive occupational stress in a variety of ways depending on the type of work they do, their coping skills and the resources available within the organisations they work in. Due to the nature of their work, social workers are bound to be exposed to lot of stressors especially those who work in community mental health teams and children and family services.

Work-related stress is therefore worth investigating. This chapter explores and discusses the levels of work-related stress and job-satisfaction among social workers selected from community mental health teams as well as from children and family services and these were analysed to determine the impacts of occupational stressors and job satisfaction on their mental health.

Questionnaires were employed to collect information on work-related stress levels, job satisfaction levels and minor psychiatric symptoms. The stress -levels and job-satisfaction scores of social workers who worked in community mental health teams were compared with the scores of social workers who worked in children and family teams using means-scores and standard deviation statistics. The scores of these two variables were correlated using Pearson correlation coefficient. In addition to this, stress-level scores, and minor psychiatric symptoms scores were also computed. Stress level scores were also correlated with job satisfaction-scores to determine the relationship between these two variables. The social workers that participated in the study were from different catchment areas in England.

Work-related stress has been highlighted as one of the major occupational concerns over the years in Europe (Cox and Rial-Gonzalex, 2004). This health issue is therefore of significant importance in terms of addressing the wellbeing of professionals, their efficiency, issues of recruitment and retention, absenteeism, and the economic costs to organisations. Professionals such as social workers who work in mental health services and children services are bound to be exposed to occupational stressors by virtue of the work they do which involves making difficulty statutory decisions. It is therefore imperative that the sources of pressures and stressors are investigated and highlighted so that strategies and policies are implemented to address the issues of work-related stress.

There are vast volumes of literature related to work-related stress hence this chapter will look at some of the available literatures. Work-related stress is associated to the dynamic interactions between a person and the work-environment (Cox et al, 2000). This perspective emphasises that stress occurs when there is a mismatch between the demands placed on individuals and their abilities to meet these demands (National Institute for Occupational safety and Health, 1999). Other perspectives have tended to claim that work-related stress is a result of a pattern of cognitive processes, emotional reactions, and behavioural responses to adverse aspects of work-content, work-organisations, and work environment (Levi, 2000). Payne (1979) considers work-related stress as a function of interaction between work-related demands, support-systems and constraints at work, while Lazarus (1999) regards occupational stress as a state that happens when the employee perceives a demand given to him or her as difficult, exceeding or threatening to his or her adaptive resources. The literature on work-related stress also cited a variety of factors that are associated to work-related stress, some of these include violence and social isolation at work, harassment, bullying, work-overload, and unsocial hours (Leighton, 1997). Work-related stress is common in occupational settings. In fact, it has been listed as the third most common in Britain according to Agnew (2002). Numerous studies have investigated work-related stress in social work, a survey undertaken by the department of social services in Hampshire County Council found out that work-related stress was attributable to the following factors: lack of enough time to do a good-job, unreasonable work, and deadlines, insufficient consultation about changes and decisions, insufficient staff support, lack of positive feedback of acknowledgement of work (Hampshire County Council, 1997). Cox et al (2000) also related work-related stress with the following factors: poor conducive organisational culture and language, poor communication, poor support for personal development, lack of organisational aims or objectives or mission statements), role ambiguity and role conflict, low participation in decision making, office work being taken at home and inflexible work-schedules. Another study in Scotland by Burglass (1996) found out that seven out of ten managers and social workers associated work-related stress to their inability to meet the needs of their users. The same study revealed that 80% of managers and field workers reported work-related stress and some attributed office-politics and lack of power as sources of work-related stress. Other factors that have been attributed to work-related stress are convert discrimination and favouritism, lack of funds or resources, clash of personalities and lack of career advancement in the workplace (Lu et al, 1999). Long hours of work, bullying, understaffing, and job insecurity have all been. associated to work-related stress (London Hazard Centre, 1996). Another study that involved four groups of staff of which one group consisted of social workers found out that social workers who worked in statutory social services did experience more work-related stress and violence than those who worked in health and welfare services (Ballock et al, 1998). It has also been revealed that social workers are likely to suffer work-related stress if they constantly deal with traumatic cases (Hilpern, 2002).

A survey cited by Davies (1999) highlighted that out of 524 social workers surveyed, 96% stated that their jobs were stressful, while 75% reported stress related symptoms and 58% felt they manifested physical symptoms of stress. McLaughlin (2001) also cited another study that involved social services staff-members who were interviewed. 49% in this study stated a severe level of work-stress. Lack of resources, low staffing levels and work-overload have also been associated to work-related stress (Kutek, 1998). Lack of support by colleagues and managers, restructuring of social services have also been reported to cause work-related stress (Penna et al, 1995). A further study of a group of mental health professionals that included social workers reported that social workers who conduct mental-health assessments usually regard their jobs as stressful (Reid et al, 1999) while another study that involved staff members from a social work-department indicated that role confusion and lack of clarity about responsibilities contributed to work-related stress and more significantly, most of the respondents stated that work-related. stress impacted adversely on work-performance and efficiency (Oynett et al, 1997)

WORK-RELATED STRESS AND JOB-SATISFACTION

Other work-related stress studies have reported negative correlation between high work stress levels and job-satisfaction and burnout (Wollcott and Belicki, 1996), however, burnout itself is:

'a condition in which long term job stress leads to mental exhaustion,
a sense of loss of personal control, and feelings or reduced accomplishment'
(Berk, 2003, P:534).

In the literature, burnout is linked to absenteeism, poor job performance and impaired health (Wright and Bonnet, 1997). The literature also reveals that an increase in stress-level leads to a decrease in job satisfaction (Spencer, 1997, Benner, 1984). Another study that investigated the relationship between work-related stress and job satisfaction reported a significant negative correlation between stress and job satisfaction (Ostroff, 1992). Other studies that involved social workers highlighted factors that do bring about job dissatisfaction in the practice of social work.

The areas highlighted above included: the way the organisations is managed, chance of promotion, rate of pay and recognition of good work (Coffey et al, 2004).

A postal survey that consisted of the General Health Questionnaire, Maslach burnout Inventory, Karasek job content questionnaire and a job satisfaction measure sent out to 610 mental health social workers in England and Wales conducted by Evans et al (2006) revealed that 237 reported high levels of stress and emotional exhaustion and low levels of job satisfaction, 111 showed. significant levels of symptomology and distress. The same survey reported that respondents felt undervalued at work, excessive job-demands, limited involvement in decision making, and unhappiness contributed to the poor job satisfaction and most of the burnout they experienced.

Those who were approved-social workers reported greater dissatisfaction.

WORK-RELATED STRESS ON HEALTH

Coffey et al (2004) explored work-related stress in children services and reported that staff who work with children and families have the highest levels of absenteeism, poorest wellbeing, highest levels of organisational constraints and low job satisfaction compared to other established occupations. It was also found out that social workers who work in children services experience the highest levels of mental health distress compared to social workers who work in two other sectors of social services in the northwest of England. The impact of work-related stress on health has been widely documented. Approximately, one in five people suffered work-related stress in 2000 according to research by the Health and Safety Executive (Agnew, 2000). Workers who experience work-related-stress suffer from a wide range of health and behavioural problems from poor mental health, backpain to excessive alcohol consumption and smoking maintains Agnew (2002). Work-related stress has been documented as the second biggest occupational health problem in the United Kingdom Gray (2000). Some of the health problem that have been associated to work-related stress include headache, muscular tension, backache and neckache, excessive tiredness, difficulty sleeping, digestive problems, high heart rate, increased sweeting, skin rashes, blurred vision, loss of motivation, poor concentration, loss of appetite, feeling of inability to cope, poor relationship with colleagues and service-users (BUPA, 2004). It is also documented that cardiovascular disease is becoming an increased risk of work-related stress in industralised countries, affirmed Kortum and Ertel (2003). High blood pressure, irritability and dizziness have also been associated to work-related stress maintains Leighton (1997) and another study carried out by Mattiasson (1990) linked chronic occupational Stress to sleep disturbance and increased blood cholesterol. Other symptoms that have been associated to work- related-stress are dryness of the mouth, urge to cry, being fidgety, frequent micturating (urination) diarrhea and nightmares (Kenworthy et al, 1992). Mental health problems have also been associated with work-related stress which Oehler et al (1991) highlighted as feeling of depression, helplessness, hopelessness, and entrapment.

Another study carried out by Professor Smith and his team at Bristol University found out that, those with high-level of work-stress reported more frequent problems with their mental health (Smith, 1999). A similar study carried out by Metcalfe et al (2003) revealed that minor psychiatric symptoms were a consequence of high-level work-related stress. Other psychiatric symptoms that have been associated to work-related stress are mood disorders, relationship problems, and low libido, low self-esteem, weight gain, guilt, loneliness and anxiety (National Institute for Occupational Safety and Health,1999, Neulfeld, 2005).

A survey sponsored by the Health and Safety Executive from August 1995 to February 1996 on self-reported work-related illnesses found out that a quarter of the respondents used for the survey reported stress, depression, anxiety, or a physical condition that was attributable to work-stress (Health and Safety Executive, 2005). Effects of work-related stress on health can be costly to professionals as well as to companies. It is documented that health care expenditures are nearly fifty percent greater for workers who report high-level of job stress (Hutman et al,2005). The cost for the companies where these professionals work is vast. For instance, in 1995 and 1996, it was reported that 6.5 million working-days were lost in Britain due to depression, anxiety, or a physical ill health associated to work related stress and the cost to employers of work-related stress was around £370 million and to the British Society about £3.75 billion (Health and Safety Executive, 2005). However, this cost is usually left to the Taxpayers to pay through the National Health Service maintain Cooper and Earnshaw (2001). The cost of work-related stress in Europe in terms of health-costs and time lost is more than 20 billion Euros highlighted Froneberg (2003).

As already discussed in the literature, many professionals are affected by work-related stress. However, the literature has revealed that certain personality traits that are more susceptible to stress compared to others. Research carried out by doctors and psychologists identified a personality type considered to be particularly at risk of stress. The term used to describe this personality is type 'A' personality (Sutton, 2000). Type 'A' personality tends to be highly competitive, restless, achievement-motivated, hyperactive, intolerant, aggressive, deeply committed to work and hostile (Nolen-Hoeksema et al, 2003, Sutton, 2000).

TACKLING WORK-RELATED STRESS

As already discussed, occupational stress has adverse effects on professionals as well as on organisations. It is therefore important that strategies are employed by organisations as well as employees to tackle work-related stress. The Chartered Institute of Personnel and Development (CIPD, 2005) suggested four approaches which organisations can employ to tackle work-related stress. One of the approaches requires organisations to audit their policies, procedures, and systems to ensure those affected by work-related stress are supported. The second approach requires the organisations to employ a person-centred model in solving problems associated with work-related stress and other psychological issues. A third approach is geared towards maximising the wellbeing of employees. The final approach suggested by the CIPD focuses on the individual level of the employee by proving him or her help such as counselling and stress management training to deal with work-related stress. Other experts have claimed that work-related stress can only be controlled successfully if both the employee and the organisations work in collaboration in taking action at three levels to tackle work-related stress which are:

1: at the primary level, stressors are identified at organisational level and actions are taken to prevent stress at work.
2: at the secondary level, where interventions are employed to help individual employees and
3: at the tertiary level assistance is provided to employees and help relieve the symptoms of work-related stress (International Labour Organisation, 2000).

The literature review also revealed that organisations can successfully improve psychological well-being and levels of absenteeism in the workplace if interventions are employed which use training and organisational approaches that are geared towards increased employee-participation in decision making and problem solving, increase support and feedback and improve patterns of communication (Michie and Williams, 2002). Organisations should also ensure that their managers are trained in stress awareness and recognition so that they will be able to detect early signs of work-related stress (Engineering Employers Federation, 2001)).

Another research result also highlighted that teaching staff skills of stress management as well as skills of how to participate in and control their work will lead to a decrease of work-related stress. Another way of tackling work-related stress by organisations is to do a risk assessment. However, 'unlike risk assessment of physical hazards, it is likely that the risk assessment on stress will be carried out at departmental or organisational level' to identify factors that contribute to work-related stress 'through management of information systems, such as sickness absence records' (Murray, 2005 p:8). This can be done by asking employees through questionnaires and discussions about various aspects of their work which place unacceptable demands on them (Murray, 2005). The Health and Safety Executive ((HSE, 2001) recommended seven specific-levels of work-environment that need to be explored in doing a work-related stress risk assessment and these are based on: (1) the culture of the organisations in terms of how it deals with issues like long working hours, (2) the demands of the work such as the volume and complexity of the work, shift work etc. (effects of exposing the employee to physical hazards and workload), (3) the control aspect of the organisation which relates to how employees are involved in doing their work, (for example control versus demands), (4) relationship at the workplace which include harassment and bulling, (5) aspect of change of the organisation in terms of patterns of management and communication to staff such as staff understanding of the reasons of change within the organisation, (6) the assessment of the role of employee to see whether the employee clearly understands his/her role, or whether the organisation ensures the employee does not have conflicting roles, (7) staff-support is assessed in terms of training and factors unique to the individuals such as peer support, manager's support, and availability of resources made available by the Organisation geared towards the acknowledgement of individual differences.

METHODOLOGY

A questionnaire was used to collect information on work-related stress, job satisfaction and minor psychiatric symptoms. To collect information on work-related stress, a tool from Booth (1985) was adapted and piloted in this work. The tool consisted of seventeen items, each item had five choices of scores from 1 (never), 2 (rarely), 3 (sometimes), 4 (often) and 5 (always). Respondents were asked to read the items and score each of them using the scale from 1 to 5 as applied to them. The seventeen items were structured to allow respondents to comment whether: (1) they cannot get their work finished in time, (2) they do not have the time to do things, as they would like them to be done, (3), they are not clear exactly what their responsibilities are, (4) they do not have enough work to occupy their mind or their time (5) too many people make demands on them, (6) they do get on with their bosses, (7) they lack confidence in dealing with people (8), they have unsettled conflicts with other staff, (9) they get very little support from colleagues or superiors, (10) they never know how they are getting on in their jobs, as there is no feedback, (11) no one understands the needs of their departments (12) their targets or budgets are unrealistic and unworkable, (13) they have to take work home to get it done, (14) they have to work at weekends to get everything done, (15) they cannot take all holidays, (16) they avoid any difficult situations, (17) they feel frustrated.

Information on job satisfaction for this work was collected by adapting the 22-item job satisfaction subscale in the Occupational Stress Indicator devised by Cooper et al in 1997. This tool was adapted from the Career Resource Centre (2005) and employed for this work. Similar method was employed by Lu et al (1999) to collect information on job satisfaction. The measurement was used for this work consisted of 22 items, each with six choices: 6 (very much satisfaction), 5 (much satisfaction), 4 (some satisfaction), 3 (some dissatisfaction), 2 (much dissatisfaction), 1 (very much dissatisfaction). The respondents were asked to scare each of the following statements according to how each applied to them: (1) the way communication and information and information flows around your Organisation, (2) your relationship with other people, (3) your feelings about the way you and your efforts are valued at work, (4) your actual job, (5) the degree to which you feel motivated by your job, (6) your current career opportunities (7) the level of your job security in your job, (8) the extent to which you may identify with the public image or goals of your Organisation, (9) the style of supervision that your superiors use, (10) the way changes and the innovations are implemented, (11) the kind of work or task that are required to perform, (12) the degree to which you feel that you can personally develop or grow in your job, (13) the way conflicts are resolved in your Organisation, (14) the scope of your job provides avenues to help you achieve your aspirations and ambitions, (15) the amount of participation you are given in an important decision making, (16) the degree to which your job uses the range of skills, which you feel, you have (17) the amount of flexibility and freedom that you have in your job, (18) the psychological feel or climate that dominates your Organisation, (19) your level of salary relative to your experience, (20) the design or shape of your Organisation, (21) the amount of work you are given to do, whether too much or too little, (22) the degree to which you feel extended in your job.

The occupational stress indicator is one of the most widely used tools and it has a component that measures job satisfaction (Keith, 2000). It is used in the detection and management of occupational stress and it has been used with occupational groups such as social workers (Bradley and Sutherland, 1995). Studies have shown that all the outcomes of stress-effects measure such as job satisfaction, mental ill-health and physical ill health have good construct validity (Cooper and Williams, 1998).

The 12-item General Health Questionnaire (GHQ) was used in this work to collect information on minor psychiatric symptoms. The 12-GHQ is a self-administered tool that is widely used to detect minor psychiatric symptoms. The tool was developed in the 1970s, initially as a 60-item tool but a shortened version includes the GHQ-30, GHQ-28, and the GHQ-12 which is the simplest one to use with consistent reliability (Montazeri et al, 2003, Lu et al, 2004). The GHQ-12 has been used. widely in occupational settings to measure and identify whether an individual suffers from minor psychiatric disorder based on psychiatric assessment (Coffey et al, 2004). In administering. the GHQ-12, the respondents were asked to rate each of the 12 items using the following scales: 0 (better than usual, not at all, more so than usual), 1 (same as usual, no more than usual,), 2 (less than usual, rather more than usual), 3 (much less than usual, much less useful, much less capable, much less able, much more than usual). The questions relating to the health of the respondents in general were: (1) have you been recently been able to concentrate on whatever you are doing? (2) have you recently lost much sleep over worry? (3) have you recently felt that you are playing a useful part in things? (4) have you recently felt capable of making decisions about things? (5) have you recently felt constantly under pressure? (6) have you recently felt that you could not overcome your difficulties? (7) have you recently been able to enjoy your normal day to day activities? (8) have you recently been able to face up to your problem? (9) have you recently been feeling unhappy and depressed? (10) have you recently been losing confidence in yourself? (11) have you recently been thinking of yourself as a worthless person? (12) have you recently been feeling reasonably happy, all things considered?

ANALYSIS AND INTERPRETATION OF RESULTS

The sample number used for this work was 24 (2 male social workers, 15 female social workers and 7 social workers who did not indicate their genders). The respondents were grouped into two sample groups. One sample group consisted of 12 social workers who worked in a community mental health team and the other sample consisted of 12 social workers who worked in children and family services. In terms of ethnicity, the respondents classified themselves in the following ways: White British=10, Black=5, Irish=1 and 8 respondents who did not indicate them ethnicities. The stress level assessments tool had 17 items with a highest possible score of 85 and a lowest possible score of 17 if all the items were answered. The questions were designed to be answered in the following way: always = 5 points, often = 4 points, sometimes = 3 points, rarely = 2 points, never = 1 point. The scores were added for all the 17 questions and the stress levels were categorised in the following way: low stress level =17-33 total points, high-level of stress = 34- 85 total points. The work-stress levels of social workers who worked in community mental health teams were compared to those of social workers who worked in children and family services.

The mean score and standard deviation of these two sets of groups of were calculated and compared. To investigate the relationship between work-stress level and job satisfaction, stress level scores were correlated to job satisfaction scores using Pearson's correlation coefficient. Job satisfaction was measured based on a tool consisting of 22 questions with a possible highest score of 132 and lowest score of 22 if all the questions were answered using the following method: Very satisfied = 17-43, dissatisfied = 44-65, satisfied = 66-87, very satisfied = 88-132, in answering the 22 questions contained in the questionnaire. This way of scoring was adapted from Mohajeri-Nelson (1999).

For the General Health Questionnaire, each of the 12 items was scored using a 4-point scale, scored from 0 to 3. The scores were added to give a total ranging from lowest score 0 (negative psychiatric symptoms) to a highest score of 36 (positive minor psychiatric symptoms). Similar scoring method was employed previously by Metcalfe et al (2003). The Likert scoring method (0-1-2-3) was employed in this work to score the GHQ items. This method has tended to produce a wider and smoother score distribution in assessing the severity of minor psychiatric symptoms and the validity of the tool itself has also been shown to be sound in nine countries, (Goldberg et al, 1997).

The total GHQ scores of each of the respondents (N=24) were calculated and correlated to work-stress scores using Pearson's correlation coefficient. This is a statistical measure that is usually used to determine the closeness of the relationship between two variables (Graham, 1999, harper, 1991). for this work, a negative minor psychiatric symptom score ranged from 0 to 14 and positive psychiatric score ranged from 15 to 36.

In comparing work-stress levels between social workers who worked in community mental health teams and those who worked in children and family teams, it was found out that social workers who worked in children and family services experienced slightly higher level of work-stress (Mean= 48.8, standard deviation = 6.8) than social workers who worked in community mental health teams (mean score = 42.4, standard deviation = 5.9).

The work stress levels of all the social workers were correlated with job satisfaction and results showed a weak negative correlation coefficient (-0.26). This value was calculated manually using the Product-moment correlation coefficient also known as the Pearson' coefficient (Graham, 1999). A correlation coefficient value of -0.26 meant that a high-level of work-related stress was associated with a low level of job satisfaction and vice versa. Some of the of factors associated to work-related stress amongst other things were time-constraints, lack of responsibilities, too much work demands, poor relationship with management, lack of feedbacks. The results also revealed that approximately 41.7 % of the sample reported that they sometimes do not have time to do things as they would like them to be done and 45.8 % reported that sometimes too many people make demands on them in their workplace and another 25% respondents reported that sometimes they do not get on with their bosses. More than half of the population sample (66%) reported that they do not get feedbacks about work done and 70.8% of respondents reported that sometimes or often they experience a feeling of frustration at their workplace.

The results from the job-satisfaction data of this study indicated that social worker who worked in community mental health teams experienced slightly higher job satisfaction (mean=78.2, standard deviation=6.2) than those who worked in children and family services (mean =76.8, standard deviation = 3.7). Only 8.3 % of the respondents reported that they were very much satisfied with their jobs and dissatisfaction was associated to the following issues: the way communication and information flowed around their Organisation (25%), the style of supervision (21 %), the ways changes and innovations were implemented (29 %), the ways conflicts were resolved in the Organisation (42 %), the prospects of their careers and that of achieving their aspirations in their jobs (25 %), involvement in important decision making ((21 %), flexibility and freedom in doing their jobs (25 %), level of salaries relative to their experiences (25 %), the amount of work given to do (42 %).

Another data that was analysed was the one gathered from the Genera Health Questionnaire (GHQ) and from this, minor psychiatric symptoms were computed and correlated to work -stress levels. The result indicated a strong positive correlation (0.89). From the results, the population-mean minor psychiatric symptom score was 18 with standard deviation of 6.7. The result also indicated that 45.8 % of the respondents reported positive minor psychiatric symptoms and other aspects of the results revealed the following: 25% of respondents reported that their concentration was less than usual, 45.8% also reported that their loss of sleep over worry was rather more than usual, 29% of the population reported that their abilities to make decision was less than usual and 33% of others reported that they felt constantly under strain much more than usual, while 16% of the respondents could not overcome difficulties much more than usual, also16.3 % of the sample reported that their abilities to enjoy normal day to day activities was less than usual, 12.5% of others reported that their abilities to face up to their problems were less than usual while 25 % reported that they felt unhappy and depressed much more than usual and 16.7% of the sample reported that they had lost confidence much more than usual and the same percentage reported that they thought of themselves as worthless much more than usual.

LIMITATION OF THIS STUDY

The respondents who participated in this study were social workers from different geographical localities, therefore this might have influenced the outcome of the results of this study. The result might also have a limitation by virtue of the use of Booth's self-report instruments used to measure work-stress level. This measure has not been used extensively in research and hence it's reliability in terms of a tool to effectively measure work-related stress. There was also a problem in trying to select a sample for this study because one organisation did not give consent to the author to carry out this research on work-related stress and job satisfaction with the staff members where the author was working as a student social worker. This is worth noting because future researchers might be faced with similar problems of finding a sample group required to undertake research activities on work-related stress and job satisfaction.

Tools such as Occupational Stress Index (OSI) (stress scale) used in this study to measure perceived stress also has a limitation as this standardised tool and others used to measure perceived work-stress limit the various intrinsic and extrinsic factors that are associated to work-related stress (Lu et al, 1999)). These self-reporting questionnaires have also been shown to inflate the observed-associations due to individuals having particular response styles that are independent of the particular concerns of a measure that might lead to biasness of their responses. (Metcalfe et al, 2003). The literature also highlighted that stress tools attempt to relate causes of stress to outcome-measures and that self-reporting measures, stressors and outcomes do frequently overlap leading to questionable values (Schafer, J and Fals-Stewart, W, 1991). It is also worth noting that individuals with effective coping skills and those with poor ones perceive identical sources of stressors differently with those with effective coping skills giving lower ratings for work-related stress levels simply because their coping skills render the stressor less overwhelming (Keith, 2000)

IMPLICATION OF STUDY TO SOCIAL WORK PRACTICE

The implication of this study to the practice of social work is immerse. This study underpins social work-practice by providing evidence-based perspectives about the relationships between work-related stress, job satisfaction and mental health of social workers. It also contributes to a body of knowledge which both employees and employers can use as sources of resource materials centered on occupational stress. A study that enhances the understanding of the relationship between work-related stress and job-satisfaction will be of significant-importance in social work especially in term of planning interventions or strategies to tackle work-related stress and by so doing, job satisfaction amongst social workers will be enhanced. It was with this hope; this study was undertaken to identify occupational stressors and job satisfaction so that strategies and policies can be put in place in social work settings to either reduce work-related stress or prevent it. The results from this study revealed that social workers who participated in it reported that they experienced work-related stress because of numerous factors which included the following: working towards a given deadline, poor relationship with managers, lack of feedback, restricted autonomy, style of supervision, the way conflicts are resolved within the organisation, lack of support and work demands to name but a few. Knowing the factors that trigger work-related stress, employers and social workers can respond appropriately to either reduce or prevent work-related stress especially in settings such as community mental health teams and children and family services where substantial levels of work-related stress exist.

Both management and staff can address the flow of communication to reduce work-related stress. Poor communication in any organisational setting is a source of work-stress, this is more so when communication channels become clogged up, leading to crisis, chaos and conflicts and leaving employees unable to discuss or talk about their work-related stress (Holden,1992). It is therefore the responsibility of employers including those who employ social workers to create the environment where communication-flow is effective and conducive for employees to discuss and talk about work-elated stress. This study highlighted issues that can create job dissatisfaction amongst social workers who work in settings such as community mental health teams and children and family services. An awareness of these issues will enable employers to create work environment and culture that will facilitate job satisfaction and staff retention. This is therefore very important because job-satisfaction is likely to lead to work-efficiency and cost-effectiveness. Employers also need to be aware that lack of staff career prospects, poor salaries, work overload, lack of flexibility and freedom lead to job-dissatisfaction amongst social workers who work in community mental health teams and children services as evidenced in the results of this study. An awareness of these factors is not enough without putting strategies and policies in place to tackle these issues so that job satisfaction and staff-retention will be enhanced. It is very important for employers to have insight into the relationship between work-related stress and staff retention because work-related stress is the biggest single factor that is responsible for staff leaving in public sector organisations (Coffey et al, 2004). It is therefore imperative that efforts are made by employers and policymakers to reduce occupational stress especially in social work settings by implementing effective policies and legislations geared towards protecting social workers' health and tackling work-related problems such as absenteeism, low morale, lack of innovation, poor performance, to name a few. From an organisational level, it is especially important that stress management becomes an integral part of all organisations that do employ social workers so that early warning signs of work-related stress can be detected so that managers can implement strategies to reduce or prevent work related stress. Organisations should take the issues of work-related stress seriously because they have a legal obligation to protect social workers from work-related stress as highlighted in a landmark case in 1996 when Northumberland County Council paid a compensation of £175,000 to a social worker who suffered nervous breakdowns as result of work-related stress (Agnew, 2002). However, it is worth noting that work-related stress is difficult to prove. To prove work-relate stress, four conditions need to be met according to Agnew (2002). One of the conditions that needs to be established is a proof that the work-related stress was caused by a breach of duty of care by the employer, another condition that needs be established is that the work-related stress was caused by the employer's negligence and not by any other factors. The third condition that needs to be established is that the employer was previously informed of the work-related stress and the final condition that needs to be met is to prove that the work-related stress was reasonably foreseeable by the employers. This implies that employers should be able to foresee if an employee is becoming susceptible to work-related stress. Examples of such susceptibility may include illness, bereavement and other major domestic crisis (Health and Safety Executive, 2005). It is therefore important that managers that employ social workers take appropriate actions to prevent work-related stress. Ways of doing this has been suggested by the Health and Safety Executive (2001) that are geared towards advising managers to: treat employees who admit to be under work-related stress with understanding, look for signs of work-related stress in the work-place which can include: loss of motivation and commitment, poor time-keeping, frequent short periods of sick-absence as well as employees having conflicts and tensions with colleagues, poor relationship with service-users/carers as well as employees making poor decisions, having diminished control of plan of work and increase in errors. Employers should also ensure that employees have the skills, training, and the resources they need in performing their duties as well as give credit to employees for their work and efforts. It is worth noting that training is important in stress-management because research has shown that formal programmes on stress management can increase knowledge about concept of stress and can also enhance self-efficacy in terms of managing stress (Bushy et al, 2004). Stress education and management courses can enhance employees' awareness about stress and can help employees develop coping skills and resilience (Gray, 2000).

The Health and Safety Executive advises that managers should: provide if possible working conditions that are flexible and variable, ensure that employees are treated fairly and consistently in the work place, ensure that bullying and harassment are prevented, ensure that an effective two-way communication systems are put in place especially during a period of change, deal quickly and thoroughly with complaints about working conditions or other work-related issues that cause stress and take action to reduce the risks.

All employers including those who employ social workers have duties of care under the Management of health and Safety at work Regulation (MHSWR, 1999) in particular to assess stress-related ill health that is work-related. Employers also have a duty under the Health and Safety at Work Act which emphasises that they should take measures to control the risks of stress-related ill health brought about by work activities (Health and Safety Executive, 2005). It is also the employers' duty to ensure that reasonable care is taken for the safety of the employees by proving a safe place and system of work maintains Murray (2005). Cooper and Earnshaw (2011) have also highlighted that employers are required through the Management of Health and Safety at Work (MHSW)Regulation 1992 to: (1) ensure that they are aware through current literature of the sources of work-related stress and how these may affect their organisation and to make sure that they assess risks of adverse mental health problems within their workforce, (2) ensure arrangements are made to put in practice the necessary preventives and protective measures related to occupational stress. Employers should also make sure that they carry out, where appropriate a health surveillance to ensure that they have adequate information and awareness about occupational risks.

One other reflective ways of promoting stress awareness in the workplace is by developing a manual of occupational stress adapted to specific occupations to enable staff who are interested in improving health safety and performance at work to use, analyse and then to combat work-related stress. Such a manual can be useful in social work especially for the use of management and staff to underpin their practice as well as to enhance their knowledge about work-related stress. Employers like Hampshire County Council (1997) conducted a study on work-related stress and from the study, it was recommended amongst other things how to reduce work-related stress. The following strategies were recommended by the council: a review of management style and culture to achieve a greater recognition of staff efforts, a better management training in communication and motivational skills and leadership, effective support programmes for employees such as training programmes, the provision of occupational health facilities, counselling support, supervision and monitoring, training programmes for staff geared towards helping them to cope with pressure and to stay health, review of workloads and training of managers to be able to work with staff on setting priorities. Another perspective of occupational stress prevention emphasises that 'employers can prevent burnout by making sure workloads are reasonable, providing opportunities for workers to take time out from stressful situations, limiting hours of stressful work, and offering social support' (Berk, 2003, p:534)).

It is important that regular stress audits are conducted in the workplace. Effective stress-audit involves incorporating qualitative measures that are capable of being re-measured over the medium and long term (Kinder,2004). It is also important for employers to be aware of aspects of work that create intrinsic and extrinsic satisfaction for the employees in order to maximise performance and output. Aspects of a job that create intrinsic satisfaction include happiness with the job, while extrinsic satisfaction relates to issues such as contentment with supervision, pay and promotion in the job (Hochwarter et al, 2001). It is worth noting that reducing work-related stress is not only the responsibility of the employers, but it is also the responsibility of the employees such as social workers to reduce or prevent work-related stress in the workplace. The literature has suggested a lot of strategies which every employee including social workers can take to reduce or prevent work-related stress at personal level. Social workers can employ strategies such as: maintaining a balance between work and leisure, managing personal workload and environment effectively, allowing emotional outlets by talking about feelings to work colleagues, allowing physical outlets such as relaxation, exercise, swimming and using counselling facilities to reduce work-related stress (Murray, 2005). It has also been recommended by Murray (2005) that every employee should make a habit of: (1) keeping a record of all dates, events, and work-related symptoms they suffer, (2) having a personal record of working hours including overtime, (3) making complaints in writing to employers about work conditions that are not conducive, (4) seeking medical advice from individual doctors and occupational health, this means that employees who are adversely affected by occupational stress can access their general practitioners to discuss these issues as well as to explore with them the feasibility of writing for them prescription of medication where necessarily to combat the effects of symptoms of occupational stress, (5) completing an incident form after an occurrence of serious bullying and harassment in the work-place. By doing the above, employees can be able to seek out help as soon as possible to address or tackle work-related stress and by so doing, they will be able to be healthy at work as well as be effective and efficient in performing their roles. Other strategies that can be employed by social workers to reduce work-related stress include learning to be assertive, prioritising tasks, delegating, and sharing responsibilities and positive thinking that is looking at each stressful event as an opportunity for improvement (Hutman et al, 2005), avoiding unhelpful responses to stress such as increased alcohol in-take, smoking, high caffeine intake (BUPA, 2005).

Another strategy social workers can use to address the issue of work-related stress is through supervision because research has shown that supervision that is geared towards a model that uses interventions that facilitate interpersonal awareness, allow for feedback and advice, ensure autonomy as well as problem solving do improve mental health in the workplace (Williams et al, 1998). Social workers can therefore advocate for this type of model in their workplaces. Another supervision model available to social workers is the one advocated by Kadunshin (1992) which uses three levels (administrative, educative, and supportive levels). This model can be adapted in the practice of social work, for instance at administrative level, managers can use supervision to ensure social workers comply with occupational policies and procedures of the agency where they work. At the educative level, supervision can be tailored so that social workers are provided information/advice that they need to know or have to do their jobs. At the supportive level, supervision can be directed primarily to supporting the workers and building their morals maintains Kadunshin (1992). Supportive supervision is important to the workers because it helps to prevent tension and stress from developing. It also reduces the impact of work-related stress as well as helps the workers to adjust (Kadunshin,1992). Research by Martininez (2004) conducted in the field of welfare services found out that group supervision contributed to reducing job stress as well as in increasing the level of job satisfaction, co-worker support and cohesion. It is therefore advisable that social workers share their work-related problems with their colleagues so that they will be able to support each other thereby enhancing the deliverance of their duties. In fact, the quality of social relationship and social support at work have been shown to influence occupational stress (Ganster et al, 1986). Studies have shown that supportive work-environment which includes co-workers, managers, team and peer cohesion and rewards can help reduce occupational stress (Lundstrom et al, 2002). Other strategies that can reduce work-related stress according to the literature include relaxation therapy, exercise, yoga, message, meditation, biofeedback therapy and cognitive behavioural therapy (Kenworthy et al, 1992, Nolen-Hoeksema et al, 2003). Relaxation helps to calm the body and the mind, and it is probably the most effective way of enabling the body to adjust to it's normal level of functioning when under stress (Williams, 1994). It has also been mentioned in the literature that one of the simplest ways to relax the body progressively is to start with the toes and slowly work up the body, relaxing each in turn (Williams, 1994). Another author called Powell (1992) illustrated how someone can progressively relax the various muscles mentioned below:

Hands and arms: start by clinching the fists and then tense the arms until you feel tightness in the hands and arms, then slowly relax them.

Shoulders: start by hunching the shoulders, then gradually allow them to settle, then slowly relax them.

Forehead: start by pulling the eyebrows together, then slowly let your face smoot out to relax.

Eyes: start by closing the eyes up tightly, then slowly let them smooth out, leaving your eyes closed, feeling your eyeballs sink and your eyelids sags downwards with no firmness.

Jaw: start by biting the molars together then slowly ease them off and let your jaw be heavy.

Back Neck: start by pulling the chin forward towards your chest and then allow yourself to feel the tightness, then slowly relax.

Front neck: start by pulling your head backwards and allow yourself to feel the tightness, then slowly relax.

Stomach: start by pulling your stomach tightly and slowly let it go and let it relax.

Thighs: start by pulling your heels down against the floor, then feel the tightness on your thighs, then slowly allow the tightness to go.

Calves: start by pointing the toes outwards and allow yourself to feel the tightness, then slowly allow the tightness to go.

Exercise has also been identified as one of the strategies that can be employed to reduce stress. It has been proven that exercises such as jogging, swimming, and cycling help to lower heartrates and blood pressure, thereby reducing stress. (Nolen-Hoeksema et al, 2003). Yoga is also a useful technique that involves mental and physical exercise which helps to enhance relaxation thereby alleviating stress symptoms. (Sutton, 2000). Another stress relieving strategy is meditation which has been shown to produce stress reduction effects (Sutton, 2000). Another intervention that can be employed to reduce work-stress is biofeedback therapy which is a process that helps individuals to identify aspects of their physiological states that are relaxed through an electronic device and these aspects are then altered leading to relaxation effects thereby reducing stress (Sutton, 2000, Nolen-Hoeksema et al 2003). Cognitive Behavioural therapy has also been shown to help individuals deal with and cope with stressful situations I Nolen-Hoeksema et al, 2003).

All the above strategies or interventions discussed in the preceding paragraphs can be used by social workers to help them reduce or prevent work-related stress. It is inevitable that social workers will experience work-related stress and will be likely off sick. When this happens, they can be helped to rehabilitate by their employers. Thomson and Neathey (2003) recommended strategies that could be employed to help employees who had suffered from work-related stress to rehabilitate. Their recommendations based on research they conducted suggested the following:

1: early contacts with the employee who is undergoing rehabilitation by a member of the organisation that employs him or her to offer support and empathy.

2: early health assessments to be instigated by referral to occupational health therapy by the end of four weeks but this can be expedited if the employee demands such an assessment.

3: accurate assessment and diagnosis of occupational stress geared towards empathy and support.

4: therapeutic intervention centred around the employee's needs.

5: gradual return to work alongside full pay for a period of time.

6: work adaptation adjustment and review of previous work role and workload, changes of how work is managed or by reducing working hours on the employee's return to work. However, it is worth noting that employees cope with occupational stress differently. Some social workers have personality trait as hardiness that enables them to sustain occupational stress, while others are more susceptible to stress (type A personality). An individual with a Hardy personality is someone who can face significant stressors but has a less likelihood of falling ill, either mentallor physically than those than those who lack hardiness (Williams, 1994). Knowledge of this literature will enable employers to treat social workers individually when they are experiencing occupational stress. This is very important because the social work profession is culturally diverse, and the way various individuals perceive occupational stress might be different. This view was highlighted by research carried out at the university of Bristol by a team led by Professor Smith. The team found out that Non-White workers reported higher levels of occupational stress than their White counterparts did, although numerically, Black workers who participated in the research were few (Health and Safety Executive, 2000). A similar result was also evident in this study. For instance, Black social workers who participated in this study reported a higher mean-stress-level of 46.3 compared to the mean stress-level of the other respondents (43.1). However, caution must be exercised because only five social workers classified themselves as Black in this study. It is therefore important in view of the changing patterns of the working force for employers to ensure that strategies are taken that are geared towards managing occupational stress with a holistic context aimed at considering issues such as social inequality, disability, and gender (Cox et al, 2004).

CONCLUSION

As already discussed in this chapter, work-related stress impacts on social workers adversely especially those who work in community mental health teams and children services. However, other social workers who work in other settings are also exposed to occupational stressor as highlighted in the literature used in this project and the results of this project. The adverse effects of work-related stress on social workers are not only detrimental to them in terms of triggering minor psychiatric symptoms but it is also detrimental to the organisations where they work in terms of economic costs. An awareness of sources of occupational stress will enable employers of social workers to initiate strategies and policies geared towards reducing work-related stress in settings where social workers work. The literature used in this study as well as the results from this study highlighted factors that do influence occupational stress which include lack of clarity of responsibility, too much work-demands, fraught relationship with managers, lack of feedbacks, tight work-deadlines and poor organisational procedures and culture in terms of how things are done within the organisation. These occupational stressors do not only impact on the mental health of the professionals adversely, but these can cause absenteeism, mental and physical ill-health, economic loss and job dissatisfaction. Some of these dissatisfactions and stressors can be reduced at organisational level by tackling issues around the way communication flows in an organisation, the style of supervision, the ways conflicts are resolved, the ways employees are given flexibility and freedom to perform their roles, the ways changes are implemented, the way career prospects and aspirations are promoted, the degree of involvement of employees in decision-making, the salary level relative to experience and the amount of work-load. At personal level, all employees including social workers, should advocate for favourable working conditions and culture to reduce or prevent occupational stress. Apart from advocating for conducive working environment and culture, all employees including social workers can also employ preventative interventions to reduce stress. Some of these interventions as highlighted in this project include doing relaxation therapies such as progressive relaxation, yoga, biofeedback therapy or by seeking help through cognitive behavioural therapy, also through supervision or co-worker support, soliciting support during rehabilitation from work-related ill-health and through medical support. However, occupational stress cannot be effectively reduced if there are no effective legislation geared towards assessment and management of occupational stress. It is therefore the responsibility of policy makers to ensure that occupational policies are enacted to reduce work-related stress in the workplace so that all employees in various occupational sectors such as social workers who work in settings such as community mental health teams and children services can perform their roles effectively without fear of suffering from occupational stressors that will lead to ill health, absenteeism, job dissatisfaction and loss of revenue in terms of human and economic costs due to work-related stress.

LEVEL OF WORK-RELATED STRESS AND JOB SATISFACTION COMPARISON BETWEEN SOCIAL WORKERS BASED IN COMMUNITY METAL HEALTH TEAMS (CMHT) AND THOSE WHO WORK IN CHILDREN SERVICES.

STRESS LEVEL (CMHT)	LEVEL OF JOB SATISFACTION (CMHT)	STRESS LEVEL CHILDREN SERVICES	JOB SATISFACTION CHILDREN SERVICES
44	80	46	85
54	75	35	80
50	79	38	71
42	70	51	77
40	73	57	76
46	76	38	78
35	71	48	71
44	75	47	74
41	90	42	78
44	80	48	77
32	81	43	76
37	90	32	79
Total=509	Total =940	Total= 525	Total = 922
Mean=42.4	Mean = 78.3	Mean =43.8	Mean 76.8
Standard Deviation	Standard Deviation	Standard Deviation	Standard Deviation
5.9	6.2	6.8	3.7

Standard Deviation scores were computed by hand

CALCULATING THE CORRELATION BETWEEN WORK STRESS LEVEL AND JOB SATISFACTION

Product-moment Correlation coefficient = (Sxy) ÷(SxSy) where Sxy is the co-variance given by the formula: (Sum of the product of scores of stress-levels and that of the scores of job-satisfactions divided by the number of items) minus (the product of the means of the two sets of scores) and for the formula is Sxy= $\sum XY \div n - \dot{X}\bar{Y}$

Sxy = -7.98

Sx is the Standard Deviation of the stress scores.

Sy is the Standard Deviation job-satisfaction scores.

Sx = Standard Deviation (Stress level score) Sx = $\sqrt{(\sum X^2 \div n)} - \dot{X}^2$

   = $\sqrt{(45536 \div 24)}$ -1857.61) = $\sqrt{(1897.33 - 1857.61)}$ = $\sqrt{(39.72)}$ = 6.30

Sy = $\sqrt{\sum Y^2 \div n}$) $-\bar{Y}^2$

Sy = $\sqrt{(145100 \div 24)} - 6021.76)$ = $\sqrt{(6045.83 - 6021.76)}$ = $\sqrt{(24.07)}$ = 4.91

Correlation Coefficient = Sxy ÷ SxSy

        -7.98 ÷ (6.30 x 4.91)

        = -7.98÷30.93 = -0.26

Correlation Coefficient = - 0.26 (negative correlation)

PERCENTAGES OF RESPODENTS WITH RESPONSES OF EITHER 'SOMETIMES' 'OFTEN' OR 'ALWAYS' TO EACH OF THE STRESS ITEMS

ITEMS	Total percentages of respondents with the answer of either 'sometimes', 'often 'or 'always' to the items
1. I cannot get my work finished in time	41.7%
2. I haven't the time to do things as I would like them to be done.	48%
3. I am not clear exactly what my responsibilities are.	29.1%
4. I haven't enough to occupy my mind or my time.	20.8%
5. Too many people make demands on me.	45.8%
6. I do not get on with my boss.	25%
7. I lack confidence in dealing with people.	16.6%
8. I have unsettled conflicts with other staff.	25%
9. I get very little support from my colleagues or superiors.	75%
10. I never know how I am getting on in my job, there is no feedback.	66%
11. No one understands the needs of my department.	70.8%
12. Our targets or budgets are unrealistic and unworkable	79.2%
13. I have to take work home to get it done.	75%
14. I have to work at weekends to get everything done.	45.8%
15. I can never take all my leave.	29.1%
16. I avoid any difficult situations.	33.3%
17. I feel frustrated.	70.8%

PERCENTAGES OF RESPONDENTS WHO EXPERIENCED SOME WORK-DISSATISFACTIONS

ITEMS	Percentages of respondents with some dissatisfactions in doing their jobs.
1. The way communication and information flow around your organisation.	25%
2. Your relationship with other people at work.	8.35%
3. Your feeling about the way you and your efforts are valued at work.	29.2%
4. Your actual job.	16.7%
5. The degree to which you feel motivated by your job.	16.7%
6. Your current career opportunities.	25%
7. The level of your job security in your job.	16.6%
8. The extent to which you may identify with the public image or goals of your organisation.	62.5%
9. The style of supervision that your superiors use.	21%
10.The way changes and innovations are implemented.	29%
11. The kind of work or task that you are required to perform.	20.8%
12. The degree to which you feel that you can personally develop or grow in your job.	29.2%
13. The ways conflicts are resolved in your organisation.	42%
14. The scope of your job provides avenues to help you achieve your aspirations and ambitions.	25%
15. The amount of participation which you are given in an in important decision-making.	21%

16. The degree to which your job uses the range of skills which you feel, you have.	37.5%
17. The amount of flexibility and freedom that you have in your job.	25%
18. The psychological feel or climate that dominates your organisation.	58.3%
19. The level of your salary relative to your experience.	25%
20. The design or shape of your organisation's structure.	58.3%
21. The amount of work that you are given to do, whether too much or too little.	42&
22. The degree to which you feel extended in your job.	37.5%

RELATIONSHIP BETWEEN WORK-STRESS AND MINOR PSYCHIATRIC SYMPTOMS

Respondents	Work stress Scores	Minor Psychiatric-symptoms scores	Stress-level score Scored.	Minor psychiatric symptoms-scores squared.	Product of scores of stress-levels and that of minor psychiatric scores
	(X)	(Y)	(X^2)	(Y^2)	(XY)
1	44	20	1936	400	880
2	54	29	2916	841	1566
3	50	32	2500	1024	1600
4	42	42	1764	225	630
5	40	12	1600	144	480
6	46	14	2116	196	644
7	35	11	1225	121	385
8	44	19	1936	361	836
9	41	13	1681	169	533
10	44	23	1936	529	1012
11	32	10	1024	100	320
12	37	14	1369	196	518
13	46	20	2116	400	920
14	35	14	1225	196	490
15	38	15	1444	225	570
16	51	29	2601	841	1479
17	57	32	3249	1024	1824
18	38	14	1444	196	532
19	48	22	2304	484	1056
20	47	20	2209	400	940
21	42	12	1764	144	504
22	48	19	2304	361	912
23	43	14	1849	196	602
24	32	9	1024	81	288
Total	1034	432	45536	8854	19521
Mean	43.1 $(\dot{X})$	18 $(\bar{Y})$			

RELATIONSHIP BETWEEN WORK-STRESS AND MINOR PSYCHIATRIC SYMPTOMS

Calculating the Pearson Correlation Coefficient:

Correlation coefficient = Sxy ÷ Sx Sy

Where Sxy is the covariance of stress scores and that of the minor psychiatric scores. The formula for this is: $\sum XY ÷ n - \dot{X} \bar{Y}$ where $\sum XY$ is the sum of the product of stress scores and that of minor psychiatric scores which is: 19521.

$\dot{X}$ represents the mean of work-stress scores which is 43.1 and $\bar{Y}$ is the mean of the minor psychiatric scores which is 18.

n is the number of respondents = 24

Using the formula $\sum XY ÷ n \dot{X}^2 \bar{Y}^2$ which represents the covariance of stress scores and that of minor psychiatric scores (Sxy)

The Covariance of stress scores and that of minor psychiatric symptoms: therefore, the formula for this is: $\sum XY ÷ n - \dot{X} \bar{Y}$

From the above formula, SxSy = 19521÷24 - (43.1 x 18) = 813.38 – 775.8 = 37.58

Standard Deviation of Stress Score: Sx = $\sqrt{\{\sum x^2 ÷ n - \dot{X}^2\}}$ = $\sqrt{\{45536 ÷ 24) – 1857.61\}}$ = $\sqrt{\{1897.33 - 1857.61\}}$ = $\sqrt{(39.72)}$ =6.30

Standard Deviation minor psychiatric symptoms: Sy = $\sqrt{\{\sum y^2 ÷ n - \bar{Y}^2\}}$ = $\sqrt{\{8854 ÷ 24 – 324\}}$ = $\sqrt{\{368.92 -324\}}$ = $\sqrt{\{44.92\}}$ = 6.7. Therefore, the Correlation Coefficient is: Sxy ÷ SxSy = 37.56 ÷ {6.30 x 6.7 } = 37.56 ÷ 42.21 = 0.89 (positive correlation)

PERCENTAGES OF RESPONDENTS WHO REPORTED POSITIVE MINOR PSYCHIATRIC SYMPTOMS TO THE ITEMS BELOW

Items	Percentages of respondents and answers give.
1. Have you recently been able to concentrate on whatever you are doing?	25% responded: less than usual
2. Have you recently lost much sleep over worry?	45.8% responded: Rather more than usual
3. Have you recently felt that you are playing a useful part in things?	20.8% responded: less so than usual
4. Have you recent felt capable of making decisions about things?	29% responded: less than usual
5: Have you recently felt under pressure?	33% responded: much more than usual
6. Have you recently felt you could not overcome your difficulties?	16% responded: much more than usual
7. Have you recently been able to enjoy your normal day-to- day activities?	16.3% responded: less than usual
8. Have you recently been able to face up to your problems?	12.5% responded: less than usual
9. Have you recently been feeling unhappy and depressed?	25% responded: much more than usual
10. Have you recently been losing confidence in yourself?	16.7% responded much more than usual
11. Have you recently been thinking of yourself as a worthless person?	16.7% responded: rather more than usual
12. Have you been feeling reasonably happy, all things considered?	25% responded: less than usual

CHAPTER TWO

LOOKING AT HOW POOR SELF ESTEEM INCREASES RISK FOR DEPRESSION IN ADOLESCENT GIRLS AND THE PRACTICAL STEPS THAT CAN BE TAKEN BY SOCIAL WORKERS TO ENHANCE SELF-ESTEEM IN YOUNG PEOPLE.

The beginning of adolescence is a transition from childhood to adulthood which extends from 12 years to the late teens maintain Atkinson et al (2000). During this transition, adolescents deal with various changes and stresses such as academic expectations, physical and emotional changes, family and peer group relationship changes alongside stresses that come along with vocational and career plans (Currie and Todd, 2003). It is therefore important that adolescents form secure and enduring sense of self because a failure to do so, will potentially lead to a sense of confusion and in extreme cases, a formation of a negative identity (Birch and Malim, 1998).

In trying to have a sense of themselves, adolescents embark on a process of evaluating themselves to establish their self-esteem, a term that refers to the way someone approves or likes himself or herself (Gross, 1992). A negative evaluation of self invariably leads to the formation of a negative self-esteem and generally, adolescent girls have a lower self-esteem than adolescent boys especially about abilities and body appearances, maintains Gross (1992). Researchers like Harter and others have found out that there is a positive correlation between poor self-esteem and depression in both middle childhood and at adolescence Bee (2000). This implies that adolescent girls are more at risk of depression than boys. It is worth noting that during the stage of childhood, the ratio of boys to girls suffering from depression is about the same but this increases to 1 to 2 during the transitional period of adolescence (Kendall,

2000). This chapter therefore aims to discuss how poor self-esteem increases the risk for depression in adolescent girls and what practical steps social workers can take to increase self-esteem in young people. The first part of this chapter will look at the formation of self-esteem in adolescents. The chapter will then progress to focus on how poor self-esteem increases the risk of depression in adolescent girls. The final component of the chapter will discuss what practical steps social workers have to take to increase the self-image of young people.

FORMATION OF SELF ESTEEM IN ADOLESCENT GIRLS

In looking at the formation of self-esteem in adolescents, it is worth mentioning the term self-concept because self-esteem is a component of this. The other two components of self-concept are self-image and ideal self (Gross, 1992). The term self-concept relates to the way an individual perceives himself or herself and ideal-self is about the kind of person an individual thinks he or she would like to be while self-esteem as already described earlier is the evaluative element of self and generally the difference between the self-image and ideal-self the lower, the self-esteem maintains Gross (1992). However, Bee (2000) referring to Harter's work stresses that the important thing about self-esteem is the degree of discrepancy between what one desires and what one has already achieved. It is also worth emphasising that self-esteem can take the form of global judgement or just relates to specific characteristics or abilities one possesses (Gross and McIveen, 1998). However, a variety of factors do influence the self-esteem of adolescents. Berk (2003) maintains that self-esteem is influenced by the context in which adolescents find themselves such as parental and social-environmental factors. In emphasising this point Berk (2003) referred to the work of Gray-Little and Carels in 1997 and highlighted the point that young teenagers who live in an environment or attend schools where their ethnic group is well represented 'have fewer problems with self-esteem' (p.384). Bee (2000) has also supported this view by claiming that culture plays an important influence on self-esteem in adolescents. For instance, if schools and communities endeavour to accept and support teenagers' heritage, they will be able to empower adolescents to develop 'a positive sense of self-worth and a secure identity' (Berk: 2000, p384).

The formation of such a matured and solid adolescent-identity progresses through four stages which James Marcia described as Identity Statuses and these comprise of (a) Identity Achievement (commitment to values, occupational goals etc.), (b) Moratorium (no specific commitments or delayed commitment to values and goals), (c), Foreclosure (adolescent forming commitments or accepting values such as those of adults without questioning such values or norms), (d), Identity Diffusion (no commitment to any values or goals) maintained Bee (2000) and Berk (2003). This concept of identity statuses propounded by James Marcia is based on the work of Erikson who felt that adolescents experience a sense of crisis in their pursuit to commit to goals and values and this transition is characterised by confusion and distress which continue until the identity crisis is resolved leading to a coherent sense of secure identity (Atkinson et al 2000). It is however worth emphasising that the concept of identity crisis in adolescents is nonexistent in certain non-western cultures especially where initiations of rites of passage are performed to allow direct transition from childhood to adulthood (Maybin and Woodhead, 2003, Bee, 2000)

HOW POOR SELF-ESTEEM INCREASES THE RISK OF DEPRESSION IN ADOLESCENT GIRLS

Poor self-esteem has been regarded as one of the factors that makes women vulnerable to depression especially when they are experiencing stressful life events (Brown and Harris, 1978). As already noted earlier, adolescent girls have lower self-esteem than boys at puberty hence they are more likely to be at risk to develop depression than boys. Inconclusive research has attributed the higher prevalence of depression in adolescent girls to psychological effects of both hormonal and physical changes at puberty maintain Angold et al, (1998) which implies that the psychological effects of attaining maturity impact on adolescent-girls and make them more at risk to suffer from depression than adolescent boys. A study by Sweeting and West (2002) highlighted this point by stating that adolescent girls' critical view of their body image such as a feeling of being unattractive puts them at risk of depression. The concern about their body images can lead adolescent girls to an excessive preoccupation with dieting and weight control that can impact on their wellbeing maintain Currie and Todd (2003). This is more evident in western culture where the cultural ideal slim body image is admired, and adolescent girls strive to have a slim body image and this desire puts too much stress on adolescents especially with the increase in body-fat during the transitional period (Bee, 2000, Fox, 1997). It is however worth noting that the concept of body image varies from culture to culture. For instance, a study involving British Ugandan students' evaluation of body shape reported that Ugandan students rated obese female figures lot more attractive that British students and in a similar study Asian -British women were reported to be more content with their body- size than White British Women (Fox, 1997). Another study that involved Black women in a Washington university reported by Fox (1997) indicated that Black women with high self-esteem and strong racial identity rated themselves as being more attracted than pictures of beautiful White fashion-models. It has also been claimed that apart from poor self-esteem, adolescent girls are more likely to face negative life-events than boys and they are more likely to respond to stressors with 'a more ruminative, self-focused style of responding to their own periods of distress', (Nolen-Hoesksema and Girgus, 1994: p438). In addition, adolescents-girls who are more passive and have a ruminative style of coping as well as those who have been abused or harassed are more at risk of suffering from depression (Nolen-Hoeskesema and Girgus, 1994). It has also been stated that adolescent-girls tend to internalise their problems or distresses and this internalisation is a deviant behaviour of dwelling on feelings and thoughts which make them more at risk of depression (Bee, 2000).

Another study by Thomas and Daubman (2001) stated that adolescent girls tend to have high self-esteem if they are happy within a relationship with a male partner and vice versa. Perhaps this can also be true in all relationships. It is therefore worth extrapolating from this study that relationship problems with cause unhappiness and increase the risk for depression in adolescent girls.

Another explanation why adolescent-girls are more vulnerable than boys to suffer from depression is related to gender roles and societal expectations. According to Nolen-Hoesksema and Girgus (1994), adolescent girls are put under too much pressure to fulfil societal expectations and these 'restrict their choices of careers and lifestyles and may find their accomplishments and talents undervalued relative to boys. The extent to which any of these social conditions contribute to the emergence of gender difference in depression is yet unclear but deserves more attention' p438.

Poor self-esteem coexisting with alcohol abuse or drug misuse will also increase the risk of depression for adolescent girls (West and Sweeting, 2003). The effects of racism on self-esteem has also been documented. Barn (2000) reported that studies have indicated that Black people's low self-esteem and low self-image is a result of 'living in a racist white society where blacks are perceived and treated as inferior leading to social and economic disadvantage' p66. Another factor that increases the risk for depression for adolescent-girls with low-self-esteem is having parents with mental illness (British Medical Association, 2002). This view is supported by a study on 11 to 16-year girls by Goodyer et al (1993) who reported that depression was the most prevalent disorder amongst mothers of depressed adolescent girls. The other symptoms of depression include depressed mood, diminished interest or pleasure, weight gain or loss, disturbed sleep, psychomotor agitation or retardation, loss of energy, feeling of worthless or guilt (America Psychiatric Association: 1994). The problem is worth noting because psychiatric disorders and particularly depression are the 'strongest predictors of suicidal behaviours (Fergusson et al, 2000, p37) during adolescence and early adulthood'. It is believed that adolescent girls are more likely to attempt suicide and boys are more likely to complete it (Brent and Birmaher, 2000). They also went on to claim that in 1998, suicide rates among 15 to 19-year-olds were 14.6 per 100,000 in boys and 2.9 per100,000 in girls. Similar research carried out by Soni-Raleigh et al in 1990 indicated that the levels of completed suicide in Asian young women was 80 percent higher than the rate for white women in the age group between 15 to 24 years cited from Barn (2001). Self-harming tendencies which co-exist with depression have also been associated to poor self-esteem in adolescents and it has been stressed that adolescent girls are more at risk than boys to deliberately self-harm (British Medical Association, 2003)

PRACTICAL STEPS TO BE TAKEN BY SOCIAL WORKERS TO INCREASE THE SELF-ESTEEM IN YOUNG PEOPLE.

As already highlighted, poor self-esteem impacts immensely on the health of young people. It is therefore crucial that professionals that work with adolescents especially social workers develop strategies geared towards improving self-esteem in adolescents. Various strategies have been suggested that can be used to improve positive self-esteem. A study by Andrews and Brown (1995) suggested that higher work status and satisfactory relationships help to improve self-esteem. To help young people achieve higher work status implies equipping them with appropriate skills and training for them to be able to get a job and income. This is very important because economic hardship impacts on self-esteem maintain Ho et al (1995). It is therefore imperative for social workers to take initiatives to facilitate employment-related programmes for young people that will equip them with skills and training necessarily to access and secure higher status jobs thereby improving their self-esteem (Department of Health and Social Services and Public Health Safety, 2009). Another way social workers can support young people is to employ a strategy geared towards interpersonal therapy which is a form of therapy that helps adolescents learn to deal with interpersonal difficulties, discord, loss of relationships and role transition (Brent and Birmaher, 2002). To help enhance a secured and matured identity, Berk (2003) suggested that young people should be provided with emotional support and freedom to explore values and goals, be offered opportunities to participate in extracurricular activities and vocational training programmes as well as to encourage them to explore their ethnicities and to learn about other cultures in a respectful manner. This means that social workers can support young people in this context to enable them to develop a more positive self-esteem that is likely to enhance a stable identity.

Another practical step that social workers can employ to increase the self-esteem in young people is to work in partnership with them to facilitate accessing facilities such as housing, leisure, and recreation. It is also important for social workers to encourage young people to participate in physical activities because evidence suggests that doing physical activities promote self-esteem.

Earlier in this chapter, it was indicated that drug-misuse, alcohol misuse, suicide and depression are associated with poor self-esteem, therefore it is important for social workers to be aware of these issues so that they will be able to take practical measures such as referring young people to appropriate community adolescent mental health services or drug and alcohol services to deal with issues of self-esteem and substance misuse. Social workers can also use assertive outreach services to link young people with mental illness and substance misuse. Discrimination and racism are positively related to low self-esteem as already evidenced in this chapter. It is therefore the responsibility of social workers to tackle issues of racism and discrimination. A model for working with Black people suggested by Sassoon and Lindon (1995) is geared towards advocacy, legal representation, Black training projects that focus on skills of consultancy to enable Black people confront racism from a recipient point of view.

Another way social workers can promote self-esteem and ethnicity is to facilitate religion and language because these are deeply rooted in ethnicity maintains Ghuman (1999). However, it is worth bearing in mind that lot of young people take the issue of religion with a lukewarm approach and generally participation in organised religion declines during the adolescence years Maintains Steinberg (1993).

Social workers also have to work in partnership with parents of young people in promoting positive self-esteem in young people because this is important because 'parent-child relationships remain vital for helping adolescents became autonomous, responsible individuals ' (Berk, 2003: p.395). Involving parents in promoting positive self-esteem in young people, social workers should be aware of various parenting styles because these have been said to affect self-esteem. The most influential model about parenting styles was proposed by Diana Baumrind (1973), which she described as: permissive, authoritative, permissive, and authoritarian parenting styles. According to Cole and Roker (2001), authoritative parents are warm and firm, set standards and hold on boundaries, give explanations and reasons with their children. Permissive parents are nurturing but communicate less and put less demands on their children while authoritarian parents are high in controlling and in maturity-demands but low in nurturing and communicate less maintains Bee (2000). In addition to the above-mentioned parenting styles, other categories of parenting have also been advocated by Maccoby and Martin but the only difference between these and Baumrind's is the introduction of another parenting style which they referred to as neglectful or uninvolved parenting style (Bee, 2000). A knowledge of the above-mentioned parenting styles by social workers will be a useful tool in organising parents-workshops geared towards Positive Parenting Styles and the generally preferred style is the authoritative parenting style, a style 'that involves the giving of warmth and affection, which is necessarily to enhance the young person's sense of self-worth and ability to interact with other people' (Coleman and Roker, 2001 p.67).

The formation of self-esteem in adolescents is influenced by parental, social, cultural, and societal factors either in a positive way or in a negative way. A negative influence on self-esteem will result in a poor self-esteem and at puberty, girls have a lower self-esteem than boys, making girls more at risk of depression than boys, about twice more likely for girls to suffer from depression than boys. The reason for this has been associated to the theory that adolescent girls are more likely than boys to be exposed to stressful life-events and they are more prone to internalising their distress and discord, while boys like externalizing theirs'. Improving self-esteem in adolescents requires the involvement of professionals like social workers and parents to tackle issues of vocation, education, racism, discrimination, housing, unemployment mental health problems, drug and alcohol misuse, social and relationship breakdowns that relate to young people.

CHAPTER THREE

IN WHAT WAYS CAN SOCIAL WORK BE REGARDED AS A PROFESSION AND DOES SOCIAL WORK REQUIRE A PROFESSIONAL STATUS?

The sociology of professions has always been contentious in that sociological perspectives had always been in divergence in attempting to justify what makes an occupation a profession. Johnson (1972) highlighted this divergence by claiming that Karl Marx related the sociology of profession to issues about 'relationship between social differentiation and class structure' but Johnson went on to add that recent sociologists have concentrated on issues of 'social mobility and forms of stratification to the exclusion of an analysis of the division of labour' (Johnson, 1972): p.10). However, the aforementioned perspectives are gradually being replaced by an attempt to look at the special attributes of what makes an occupation a profession maintains Johnson (1972). The aim of this chapter therefore is to employ sociological perspectives to discuss the sociology of profession and to argue whether social work can be regarded as a profession and whether a professional status is desirable for social work or even for social workers. The first part of this chapter will focus on sociological perspectives in trying to define a profession and the second part will advance arguments to justify whether social work is a profession, and the final part of this chapter will provide a discussion on whether a professional status is desirable for social workers or even for social work practice and how this professional status will affect social work practice.

WHAT IS A PROFESSION? SOME SOCIOLOGICAL PERSPECTIVES

Various sociological theories have been used to define a profession. Johnson (1972) argues that models used to define a profession have tended to be abstract and such theoretical statements about the definitions of a profession have been restricted to discussions and the exposition of the characteristics of a profession. One such approach used to define a profession is that of the trait perspective. This school of thought stresses the importance of listing the characteristics of an ideal typical traditional profession against which occupational groups could be compared to be a profession (Macdonald, 1995). In listing the attributes or traits of a profession, sociologists managed to come to a convergence in distinguishing the characteristics of a profession maintains Jackson (1970). The distinctive core traits which an occupation needs to possess to qualify for a professional status have been taken from the work which Millerson did in 1964. In highlighting Millerson's core traits, Johnson (1972) commented that these core traits were taken from not less than twenty-one authors who attempted to list the essential elements of a true profession. The most commonly mentioned traits which an occupation needs to have to be a profession according to Johnson (1972) include the following: {a) skills based on theoretical knowledge, (b) existence of training and education specifically for the profession, (c) presence of strategies for evaluating competencies of members (d) existence of a professional organisation (e) code of conduct adherence and (f) an altruistic service.

Other sociologists belonging to the school of functionalism have also contributed to the sociology of professions and their perspectives flourished in the sociology of professions until the 1960s maintains MacDonald (1995). The influence of functionalism on the sociology of professions was largely due to the work of Durkheim on the ethnics of the professions in the late 1950s argues MacDonald (1995). The proponents of functionalism include sociologists such as Bernard Barber and Talcott Parson maintains Johnson (1972). The central focus of this paradigm of functionalism stresses on professional behaviours in trying to determine what makes an occupation a profession. Four essential attributes have been advanced by functionalists in determining a profession and these are: (a) high degree of generalised and systematic knowledge, (b) an orientation to community interests rather than self-interests, (c) a standard of behaviour monitored by code of ethics and (d) an honorary and monetary reward systems (Johnson, 1972).

Another sociological model that has also contributed to the sociology of professions is symbolic interactionism. This approach stresses on the actions and interactions of individuals and groups and how they make their social worlds as participants as well as how they develop their careers asserted MacDonald (1995). This concept of sociology originated from the Chicago school of sociology and proponents of symbolic interactionism emphasise on the circumstances of people in an occupation in trying to turn their occupation into a profession and themselves into professionals as well as how they negotiate and maintain their special position (Robert, 2003). However, some sociologists have questioned the relationship between professional status and power. Answers to this question has led to two schools of thought. One of these schools stresses that professionals have an 'enormous power over the state policies and the personal affair of individuals' (Freidson, 1994, p31). He went on to maintain that by registering and employing other exclusive devices, the professionals create an artificial dependence of their skills and monopoly of their ideology (Freidson, 1994). This means that the relationship between professionals and their clients is asymmetrical in nature. The second school of thought disagrees with the preceding view. For this school of thought, the professionals are the passive instrument of the state and that they have little influence on others suggested Freidson (1994). He went on to point out that the professionals are merely performing their roles to the requirements of their masters and in so doing, their professional power diminishes (Freidson, 1994). In other words, professionals tend to form a close relationship with the state in performing their roles.

The sociology of professions has undergone a dynamic process. As time has elapsed, and societies have become more industralised and cosmopolitan, professionals have undergone a process of change in terms of their characteristics or traits. The process of change is regarded as professionalisation and according to Larson (1997), it is a process through which professionals sought to control the market of their expertise and how they strive to attain upward collective social mobility.

In trying to define a profession, Johnson (1972) distinguished between a profession and professionalisation. He defined a profession as a means of controlling an occupation while he regarded professionalisation as a specific process through which certain occupations must undergo at a particular time in their history (Johnson, 1972). One aspect of professionalisation that has to be stressed is the gender relation of patriarchy. This is worth highlighting because the patriarchal nature of traditional institutions provided the 'backdrop for professional projects which placed severe constraint on women's ability to engage in such projects' (Witz, 1992: pp. 67-68). It has been evident from history that men have been dominate over women in traditional professions. It is therefore worth recognising and addressing the concept that collective actors engaged in professional projects are 'positioned not only within class relations but also within gender relations of dominance and subordination in the gender relations of patriarchy' (Witz, 1992: pp. 67-68).

As already noted from the sociological perspectives employed in this chapter, a profession has been associated to a distinct body of knowledge and skills while other ways of defining a profession focus on the traits of occupations. However, to augment the understanding of the concept of a profession, the penguin English dictionary edited by Allen (2002) regarded a profession as an occupation that possesses a specialised body of knowledge as well as a requirement for an intensive academic preparation.

The features of a specialised body of knowledge in the sociology of professions is important especially in industrial societies because of the benign view that expect knowledge is 'priced' and therefore, it is needed for society to function property (Baldock et al, 2003 p.243).

ARGUMENTS TO JUSTIFY THAT SOCIAL WORK IS A PROFESSION

The debate whether social work is a profession has prevailed for a long time. Meyer (1970) stresses this point by stating that since Abraham Flexner in 1915 posed the question whether social worker is a profession, many social workers have tried to demonstrate that social work is a profession while others have not committed themselves to this bandwagon. Proponents of the idea that social work is a profession had made their claim a long time ago, for instance, as long as 1942, it was fairly evident that social work had progressed far in the direction of a professional status argues Brown (1942), a view supported by Seed (1973) who noted that the British Federation of Social Workers was concerned about the promotion of professional interest of their practice as far as the 1930s. As time has progressed, Social Work has persevered to have a professional status and to undergo a process of evolution and there has been a gradual shift of professionalisation during the 25 years after the end of the war (Lymbery, 2001). Recently, there has been an emphasis on university degree-training-programmes for social work qualification, which are geared towards professionalisation.

The professional status of social work can therefore be justified by referring again to the trait perspective mentioned earlier in this chapter. As ready discussed this perspective focuses on characteristics which an occupation should possess to qualify for a professional status. Using the trait perspective, it appears that social work is associated with a special body of knowledge and skills and although social work borrows knowledge from the social and behavioural sciences, it however uses this knowledge and skills in a unique approach and 'the way in which social work utilises basic knowledge of human behavor and social systems is what gives social work its stamp' (Meyer, 1970: p.26). Another argument that justifies the professional status of social work is related to the concept of values. It is argued that to profess a special body of knowledge and expertise implies espousing a set of values which are supposed to be promoted for the benefit of the profession and the service-users maintains Baddock et al (2003). Social work in this sense has not only espoused a set of values but has made a commitment towards these values and according to the British Association of Social Workers (2003), social work is committed to five basic values which are centred on human dignity and worth, social justice, service to humanity, integrity, and competence.

As a requirement for social work qualification, it is expected that social workers have to be competent in communicating and engaging with service users, should also be able to assess and identify needs of service-users and plan strategies or interventions (Care Plans) to meet the needs identified as well as be able to evaluate care-plans mutually agreed with service-users.

Apart from it's association with specialist knowledge and specific skills and values, social work has also gained credence by the upgrading of the social work- qualification to degree level.

There has also been a restructuring of educational and training programmes that started from the time of the General Social Care Council progressing to the period of the Health and Care Professions Council now in consultations with Social Work England to take over the responsible of regulating social workers as well as formulating standards and values and a code of practice for social workers in England. The Genera Social Care Council formally closed in August 2012. Apart from the above checks and balances, the British Association of Social Workers (BASW) also expects all it's registered members to ensure adherence to the code of ethics in their practice in safeguarding and promoting the rights of service-users (BASW, 2003).

Another trait which occupations needs to possess to qualify for a professional status is altruism. To justify whether social work has an altruistic value, it is necessarily to look at the definition of altruism. This has been defined as an 'act performed for the sake of another person without any personal gain' (Gross, 1992: p432). It can then be argued that social work from it's history of philanthropy has always been associated with altruism in the sense that social work has always been about helping others and it is for this reason that young people go into social work for 'a genuine desire' and 'to make a difference', while mature people join social work 'to put something back in' either as professionals or volunteers (Douglas and Philpot, 1998: pp49-50).

To have a professional association and a code of conduct are two of the traits of a profession. Social work in this respect can boast of having a national code of practice which was first launched by the General Social Care Council in September 2002 for care workers and employers (GSCC, 2002) but an oversight of this was subsequent taken over by the Health and Care Professions Council who are also in the process to hand-over this responsibility to Social Work England who will then be responsible for keeping a register as well as setting professional and educational standards alongside ensuring social workers are fit to practise.

Having employed the trait-perspectives in justifying the professional status of social work, one can argue that social work possesses all the traits of a profession which include possessing: skills based on theoretical knowledge and science, specific training, and education for the profession of social work, strategies for evaluation of competences, a code of conduct, a body that regulates the profession as well as possessing an element of altruism.

REASONS WHY SOCIAL WORK AND SOCIAL WORKERS NEED A PROFESSIONAL STATUS AND THE IMPLICATION OF PROFESSIONALISM TO THE PRACTICE OF SOCIAL WORK

The final component of this chapter provides a discussion of whether a professional status is desirable for social workers and how will this influence social work practice. It is important if a profession wants to be recognised by society to demonstrate efficiency and competency in the delivering of services which it claims to provide. In this respect, it is very important for social workers and social work to attain a professional status especially when social work and its professionals are usually bashed by the press and the media when issues related to their practice go wrong because historically there has been a tendency for the media and the press to bash social workers in 'highly published examples of poor practice, particularly in the child protection field and the abuse of vulnerable individuals by those caring for them' (Dominelli, 1997, P.1). It is therefore imperative for social work to have a professional status because a state like Britain needs specialised knowledge and skills. As society becomes more sophisticated and industralised, it becomes very important to have available a variety of specialised knowledge and skills to compensate for the increase in diversity, 'expanding market exchange' and 'complex industrial production' as well as to cater for the increase in the variance of needs of its citizens (Reuschemey, 1986, p.105). The State for instance can use the expert knowledge and skills of social work professionals in areas related to policy making and decision making that concern the welfare of the citizens. To cater for this professionalism, it is important for the government to put something back into the profession of social work to enhance its professional status.

It is very important for social workers to have a professional status because this will give them power, social status, reward and higher market position and it is for this reason that there is a lot of tension in the pursuit of professionalism. Sometimes, this tension can be merely 'a pursuit of objective knowledge for its sake' (Jackson, 1970, p.5).

As already discussed, professional status coupled with expert knowledge will form a basis for 'collective organisations' which can be a wonderful bargaining strength (Reuschemey, 1986: pp106-107). Social workers can utilise this power through their respective professional groups to advocate for better policies relating to the social work profession. A profession such as social work is inherently bureaucratic and hierarchical in nature therefore it is advisable to use this collective bargaining power to facilitate individual career development, promote fairness, fight against discriminatory practices, ensure social justice and help fight poverty.

For social workers to be able to use their professional status to practise, they need to have the legitimate power to do so or the authority to practice and this 'rational legal authority' as termed by a German sociologist, Max Weber is the 'authority that comes from the rights and responsibilities' of the position occupied by professionals that have 'followed laid down procedures and recognised by subordinates', (Baldock et al, 2003, p.237). Being a social worker involves having a rational legal authority legitimating you to practise social work. It is therefore advisable for the state to be an influential mediator in protecting the authority given to professionals to protect the public and at the same time ensure that the process of professionalism is not based on a closure culture thereby excluding others.

There has been a move to protect the professional status of social work in England and Wales. A legislation called 'protecting of title of social worker' was passed that was geared towards safeguarding the usage of the title of social worker hence since 1 April 2005, it became an offence for someone to call himself or herself a social worker (Department of Health, 2003b)unless true.

With all the above-mentioned mechanisms which social work has: a register, a code of practice, a code of ethics, a degree training programme leading to a qualification in social work will only enhance the professional status of social work thereby equipping them with expert knowledge and skills as well as ethnical values required to practise professionally in their decision-making, the way they behave and communicate to service-users and their carers as well as to other professionals. Professionalism will also prepare social workers to be aware of discriminatory practices related to racism, ageism, religion, disability, and sexual orientation and be able to promote good anti-discriminatory practices in all aspects of their practice while performing their roles as social workers.

In concluding this chapter, it is important to stress that the debate whether social work is a profession will continue but it is plausible to describe social work as a profession as it possesses the traits of a professions, and this professional status is important for social work practice because professionalism will promote good practice based on scientific evidence as well as accountability. For those who have a contrary view will just have to take account of the changes that have taken place in the practice of social work, and they will realise that social work has reached a historic period of professionalisation.

CHAPTER FOUR

SOCIAL WORK SKILLS: ROE VERSUS WADE, THE TEA PARTY AND THE MAGNA CARTA

There are certain skills social workers are expected to have to be able to practise effectively. These skills involve the following:

1: Communicating and engaging with service-users.

These are skills that relate building of relationships which is the initial stage of working the service-users 'many of which have experienced rejection and discrimination in other parts of their lives' (Karban, 2011, pg. 183). Communicating and engaging with service-users or their relatives, families or carers is usually geared towards gathering information from them or to identify the needs of the service-user or his or his carer. The language employed to communicate and engage with service-users should be simple and not full of jargons. For those Service-users, whose first language is not English, efforts should be made to have an interpreter present in communicating with them so that an effective flow of communication can happen. Communicating and engaging with service-users can also involve the writing of letters as well as making telephone calls to either make appointments or just to talk or inform the service-users about events or interventions undertaken relating to their care-plans. In communicating and engaging with service-users, it is always advisable to ensure professional boundaries. Trevithick (2000) advises that 'good communication-skills, particular listening and interviewing skills, are essential within social work', pg53. Listening is a useful tool of communication as it helps social workers to acquire and evaluate information, empathise, and appreciate the speaker advised Trevithick. (2000).

2: Assessment and Care-Planning.

Both processes of assessment and care-planning are very important for social workers as these tasks can be statutory requirements bestowed on them For example, social workers are sometimes expected to conduct a needs assessment as per the Care Act 2014 to identify needs (social, physical, and mental) and then determine the impact of these on the ability of a service -user to achieve outcomes thereby impacting on his or her wellbeing. According to the Department of Health (2018), the expected outcomes are the following:

1: Managing and maintaining nutrition.
2: Maintaining personal hygiene.
3: Managing toileting needs.
4: Ability to be appropriately clothed.
5: Maintaining a habitable home environment.
6: Being able to make use of the home safely.
7: Ability to develop and maintain family or other personal relationships.
8: Accessing and engaging in work, training education or volunteering.
9: Making use of necessary facilities or services in the local community including public transport and recreational facilities or services.
10: Carrying out any caring responsibilities an adult has for a child.

Wellbeing according to the Department of Health (2018) constitutes the following:

1: Personal dignity,
2: Physical, mental, and emotional wellbeing.
3: Protection from abuse and neglect.
4: Autonomy over day-to-day activities including care and support that is provided to an adult.
5: Participation in work, education, training, or recreation.
6: Social and economic wellbeing.
7: Domestic, family, and personal relationships.
8: Suitability of living accommodation.
9: Individual's contribution to society.

It is always advisable to inform the service-users the aim of the assessment and the expected outcome once the assessment is concluded. In certain instances, the service-users might request for a copy of the assessment conduced on them hence it is important for them to have a copy of the assessment. Social workers should always endeavour to discuss the critical issues of confidentiality and try as possible to solicit consent from the service-users prior to the commencement of the assessment. It is always good practice to explain the issue of confidentiality to them at the beginning of the assessment and then solicit their consents (written) and stress to them that confidentiality can be broken if the person being assessed is at risk or the public is at risk. It is worth bearing in mind that assessment involves the follow: direct observation, examining existing records and files, gathering information from other professionals and agencies to identify needs (O'Hagan, 1996). It is imperative for social workers to be aware of the singularity and totality of service-users in assessing their need as every service-user is unique in terms of ethnicity, religion, sexual orientation, and age. It is also important to talk to carers as well as relatives during the process of assessment, but consent is required form the service-user especially those who those who have capacity (ability to process and retain inform alongside the ability to weigh the consequences of one's behaviour). It is worth noting that carers can request for assessments. It is also a statutory requirement for agencies to conduct a carers' assessment. There have been lot of legislations that advocate the rights of carers one example of these is the Carers (equal opportunities) Act 2004 and community care directives require local authorities to involve service-users and the Carers in the process of assessment and care planning (Department of Health 2004).The Carers (equal opportunities) Act 2004 applies in England and Wales as this Act defines a carer as someone who provides or wants to provide substantial amount of care and support on a regular basis for another individual over 18 who is in need of care and support because of mental illness, physical illness, disability or age (Social Care Institute for Excellence, 2007). During the process of assessment, good interpersonal skills are useful to have a better understanding of what is being discussed and these can include: 'questioning, clarifying, listening, empathising, reflecting, sustaining, restating, summarising, and non-verbal communications' (Campbell, 1986 p.70.). However, it is worth noting that body-language can constitute non-verbal form of communication, and this varies from culture to culture. For example, in certain African culture, the lack of eye-contact can be a sign of respect especially when the attender (the person speaking) is older and higher in status with reference to the person listening, but lack of eye-contact may be misconstrued in western cultures as being a sign of not paying attention or a sign of lying.

In the process of care-planning, it is important for the service-users to be central in the stating of goals/aims of their care-plans. For example, the service user might prefer direct payments which are cash payments to service-users to meet eligible assessed needs instead of the provision of community services. The process of putting the service-user in charge of his or her care-plan is regarded as personalisation. Houson (2010) looked at 'personalization' using a theoretical framework in particular the implication of Axe Honneth's work in four arears in which social work is regarded: (a) as care, (b) as symbolic interactions and (c) as validation and he went on to state that 'personalization' brings in focus the theme of homo economicus, the view that the actor (service-user) is rational, individualistic, utilitarian, calculative and instrumental in self-determination. This view is very important especially for service-users with capacity. The Social Care Institute for Excellence (2007) suggests that a plan should contain some of the following:

1: what the service user wants to achieve with his or her care and support, his or her goal and aspirations for the future.

2: what is important to the service user about how he or she lives his or her life, what he or she enjoys doing, his or her interests or likes and dislikes.

3: How best to support and involve the service user in decision-making.

4: Essential information for continuity of care and support for use in emergency.

5: Roles and responsibilities of professionals involved in the provision of care and support to the service-user so that the service-user receives coordinated care and support to meet his or her needs.

6: where a service-user lacks capacity to express his or her choices, have others interested in the care and support of the service-user been consulted?

7: The outcomes the service-user wants, and have other options been considered and the associated risks and benefits of each option?

8: Evidence of systems for reviewing care and support plans.

MIND (2018) also suggests that a care and support plan should set out the following:

1: What the needs of the service user are.

2: What the personal outcomes of the service-user.

3: What the Local Authority will do to meet the needs of the service-user and help achieve his or her outcomes.

4: How the Local Authority will monitor how the service-user is achieving his or her outcomes.

5: The arrangements for reviewing the care-plan information of direct payment if this is how some or all the service-user's care and support are going to be provided.

Some mental health service users who use specialist services are usually on the Care Programme Approach (CPA) care plans. The CPA was a consequence of government legislation in 1990, the beginning of the shift to community care precipitated by economic pressure on state services provision (Alcook, 2003). The shift also brought about the concept of mixed economy which created the separation between the purchasers and providers and helped to link private and public sectors services by means of contracting services (Knapp, et al, 1997). Community care when it was introduced was meant for service-users with severe* mental health problems, and it consisted of the following according to the Department of Health (2007):

1: Systematic arrangements for the assessment of the health and social needs of people accepted into specialist mental health services.

2: A care-plan which identifies the health and social care that is required from a variety of providers.

3: The appointment of a key worker (care coordinator) to keep in close touch with the service-user and to monitor and coordinate care.

4: Regular reviews and if required agreed changes to the care plan.

*Please note that the term severe mental impairment and severely mentally impaired are omitted in the Mental Health Act 1983 as amended 2007. Please also note that the aforementioned act introduced Community Treatment Orders and introduced the definition of "Mental Order' to mean any 'disorder' or 'disability of the mind' and 'mentally disordered is construed accordingly'. Approved Social Worker (ASW) replaced by Appropriate Mental Health Professional.

Section 117 aftercare of the mental health 1983 as amended 2007 is a framework that is put in place to provide care and support for discharged service users who had been detained under the following sections: 3, 37/4I (hospital order with restriction), 47/49 (transfer to psychiatric hospital with restriction of someone serving a sentence of imprisonment and 48/49 (transfer to psychiatric hospital of a prisoner who has not been sentenced from a remand prison or setting with restriction). Section 48 of the Mental Health 1983 as amended 2007 relates to the transfer of categories such as remand prisoners, civil prisoners and immigration detainees to hospital for treatment by the Secretary of Justice if the Secretary of State is satisfied by the reports of at least two psychiatrist that the prisoner or detainee to be transferred to hospital suffers from a mental disorder of a degree or nature which makes it appropriate for the prisoner or detainee to be detained in hospital for psychiatrist treatment. If the Secretary of State imposes a transfer direction in respect of persons awaiting trial or sentencing in the Crown Court, and persons remanded in custody by a Magistrate's Court, they must also impose restriction direction regarded as section 49 of the Mental Health Act 1983 as amended 2007, which imposes the same restrictions as an order under section 41. Restriction directions are discretionary with reference to civil prisoners and immigration detainees (HM Prison & Probation Service, Ministry of Justice, 2020).

Section 37 of the Mental Health 1983 as amended 2007 applies to England and Wales. This section is for Mentally Disordered Offenders convicted with an imprisonable offence but may be ordered by the Criminal Courts (Crown Courts, Magistrates' Courts) to psychiatric hospital for treatment rather than imposing prison sentence (HM Prison & Probation Service Ministry of Justice (2020). The Crown Court may also impose a restriction direction (section 41 of the Mental Health Act 1983 as amended 2007) under section 37 to protect the public from serious harm. A Magistrate's Court cannot impose a section 41 order, but if this is considered, instead of imposing a section 37, the offender will be committed to a Crown Court for restrictions to be considered. The restriction Order (section 41) lasts as long as the Hospital order except where the restriction order is discharged (HM Prison & Probation Service, Ministry of Justice, 2020).

Although a service user who is under a restriction order, is managed by the Responsible Clinician who for example will grant the service user a leave of absence from hospital, the Responsible Clinician has to seek consent from the Ministry of Justice.

Section 45A of the Mental Health Act 1983 as amended 2007 relates to a hospital direction and limitation direction considered by the Crown Court when an offender who has committed an imprisonable sentence, but the Crown court decides that it is appropriate to divert the offender to a Psychiatric hospital for treatment when the Crown Court is satisfied with the reports of at least two Registered Psychiatrists that the offender is suffering from a mental disorder of a nature or degree which makes it appropriate for the offender to be detained in hospital for psychiatric treatment and such a treatment is available (HM & Probation Service, Ministry of Justice, 2020).

If an offender who is subjected to section 45A of the Mental Health Act 1983 as amended 2007 was given an indeterminate sentence for the protection of the public or a discretionary life sentence, the limitation direction will remain in effect for the duration of detention of the offender in hospital, even past the minimum term or tariff period. The release date for such sentences is not fixed and is determined by a direction to release by the Parole Board and they will not consider release until the tariff expire date and the case will not be referred to them while the service user remains detained under the Mental Health Act 1983 as amended 2007, until the tribunal decides that, but for the limitation direction, the service user is suitable for discharge (HMP & Probation Service, Ministry of Justice, 2020).

Section 47 of the Mental Health 1983 as amended 2007 relates to sentenced prisoners who are about to be transferred from prison to hospital by the Secretary of State for treatment and for such a transfer to occur, the Secretary of State must be satisfied with the reports of at least two registered psychiatrists that the prisoner is suffering from a mental disorder of a nature or degree which makes it appropriate for such prisoners to be detained in hospital for treatment. The Secretary of State for Justice may impose restriction direction under section 49 of the Mental Health 1983 as amended 2007 which imposes the same restrictions as an order under section 41 of the aforementioned Act (HM Prison & Probation Service, Ministry of Justice, 2020).

If the prisoner is still in hospital, the restrictions will expire at the point of the automatic release date and such a prisoner will then be managed solely by the Responsible Clinician with no input from the Secretary of State as unrestricted patient and such a situation is referred to as 'national section 37' (HM Prison & Probation Service, Ministry of Justice, 2020)

The fundamental principles of the Mental Health Act 1983 as amended 2007 are as follows:

1: Respect of service-user's past and present wishes and feelings.
2: Respect for diversity, generally including diversity of religion, culture, and sexual orientation.
3: Less restriction on liberty.
4: Involvement of service-users in care-planning and delivery of services and treatment appropriate for them.
5: Avoidance of unlawful discrimination.
6: Treatments should be effective.
7: Acknowledgement and reflection of views of carers and other interested parties.
8: Service-users' safety and wellbeing.
9: Safety of public.

In June 2022, the Mental Health Act Reform Bill was published and eventually this Act will be used to amend the 1983 Mental Health Act. The principles and thymes in the proposed Mental Health Act Reform Bill include the following:

- Autonomy of service-users and their choices should be respected.
- Less restrictive practices, ensuring the Act's powers are used in the least restrictive way.
- Ensuring the definition of Mental Disorder is no longer used solely to detain service-users because they have learning disability, or they are autistic.

- The Act is only used where a person is a genuine risk to his or her own safety or that of others' and the aim should be geared towards a therapeutic benefit for the service user.
- Better support to service users including offering the option of an independent mental health advocate and allowing service users to choose their own 'nominated person', rather than an assigned 'nearest relative'.
- A 28-day time limit for transfer from prison to hospital for acutely ill prisoners and ending the temporary use of prisons for those awaiting assessments and treatments.
- A new form of Supervised Community Discharge that will allow the discharge of restricted service users into the Community, ensuring they have the appropriate care and supervision to manage the risks they pose in the community.
- Increased frequency which allows service users to make appeals to Tribunals when they are detained, and powers given to Tribunals to recommend aftercare services to be put in place.
- There should be a statutory care and treatment plan for all detained service users.
- The Service User should be viewed in a holistic way.

A portion of the first part of The Care Act 2014 should be geared towards the following principles in the provision of care and support to service-users:

1: Promoting the wellbeing of service-users.
2: Preventing, reducing, or delaying the presentation of needs that require care and support.
3: Promoting integration of care and support with health care services.
4: Providing of information and advice.
5: Promoting diversity and quality in the provision of services.
6: Cooperation between Local Authorities and relevant partners in the provision of care and support for service-users and carers.
7: Cooperation in specific cases, that is if a Local Authority requests the cooperation of a relevant partner or another Local Authority that is not a relevant partner to provide care and support to meet the needs of a service-user or carer or a carer of a child, then the relevant partner or Local Authority should cooperate except cooperating would be incompatible with it's own duties or would otherwise have an adverse effect in exercise of his functions.

3: Intervention, implementation, and provision of services.

Adams (2007) advises that an intervention relates to using different methods to enable a person to change his or her life and in certain instances this can involve using the law to protect someone from harm to self or to others or sometimes even a surgical intervention for instance a hip-replacement Interventions can also be associated to approaches such as cognitive behavioural work, counseling or advocacy, crisis and task centred work maintains Adams (2007). During the process of Intervention, vast knowledge of the appropriate resources or services (statutory or voluntary) available in the community where the assessed service-user lives is very important to enable the social worker to match the service-user's needs to achieve the required outcomes. A theoretical framework should also guide the social worker in determining the intervention he or she takes. For instance, a 'person centred approach' that is based on the idea that individuals have within themselves vast resources for development, which can be facilitated by a practitioner. The conditions for such a development depend on the practitioner's ability to be at congruence with the service-user and to be able to empathise and embrace the service-user with unconditional positive regard (Mearns and Thorne, 1998). In certain instances, the intervention undertaken by the service-user might be geared towards the recovery model which is aimed at improving a person's ability of life and social functioning by helping the person to develop his or her daily skills so that the person will be able to cope with the symptoms and the associated difficulties (Ramsay et al, 2001). Interventions can also be a process of the managing.

These are skills social workers are expected to have in performing their social work roles. Interventions are also about actions or strategies social workers employ to meet the goals or objectives stated in the care plans of service-users.

In the other hand, the process of implementation relates to carrying out the aims and objectives stated in a care plan. This requires vast knowledge of the appropriate resources or services (statutory or voluntary) available in the community where the assessed service-user lives to match the service-user's needs to the appropriate service he or she needs. In certain instances, the implementation process might be geared towards the recovery model which is aimed at improving a person's ability of life and social functioning by helping the person to develop his or her daily skills so that the person will be able to cope with the symptoms and the associated difficulties (Ramsay et al, 2001). Other processes of implementation of the care plan in social work can be referring service-users to appropriate services, helping and supporting service-users to meet their housing and employment needs as well as ensuring that they are social included in the community where they live as well as supporting them with their schooling to ensure they meet their identified learning outcomes or sorting out social welfare benefits and ensuring that service-users' awards of benefits are maximised as per their rights. Managing risks and evaluation of these can also be processes of implementation of care-plans in social work especially for children who are at significant risk of harm and abuse. Liaising with other professionals to meet the needs identified in the care plans of service-users can also be a process of intervention for social workers.

4: Promoting and enabling service-users.

The concept of enabling a service-user is about empowering him or her to maximise his or her autonomy in terms of self-determination. Adams (2007) maintains that empowerment is about partnership between the service user and the professional and this partnership should focus on the rights of the service-user which can also include the right to take risks. Empowering service-users is also about personalisation or about service users making their own decisions. The principal component of personalisation is underpinned by Self-actualisation. Sometimes empowering a service-user also involves advocating for the choices, Rights and, Freedoms of a service- user which can lead to issues of making ethical decisions as a social worker that relate to the autonomy of the service-user and the duty of care of the social worker who is supporting the service-user. The Case law of Roe versus Wade is a classical example of ethical issues relating to the autonomy and self-determination of a woman to undergo an abortion and the state's duty of care to ensure the safety and wellbeing of the unborn child. For an insight into the case law of Roe versus Wade, you must go back as far as 1969 when a 25-year-old woman called Norma McCorvey who used the pseudonym 'Jane Roe' became pregnant with her third child and she filed in a case in Dallas County Court, requesting the Court to allow her to perform an abortion claiming she was raped. At that time in Texas abortion was unconstitutional except where the mother's life was in danger. Acting for the District Attorney for Dallas County was 'Henry Wade' hence the case law Roe versus Wade. In 1973, this case made it to the Supreme Court where Ms. McCorvey's case and that of another 20-year-old Georgia woman were heard and these cases were subsequently rejected by the Supreme Court and these women were legally forced to give birth. The supreme Court argued that abortion laws in Texas and Georgia went against the United States' constitution because they infringed on a woman's rights to privacy protected by the 14th Amendment of the Constitution. On January 22, 1973, by a vote of 7 to 2, the Court Justices ruled that governments lacked the power to prohibit abortions, concluding that a woman's Right to terminate pregnancy is protected under the United States' Constitution. The above case created the 'Trimester' systems which allowed:

- an absolute Right to an abortion in the first three months (Trimester) of pregnancy
- some governments regulations to allow abortion in the second trimester.
- some states were allowed to restrict or ban abortions in the last trimester as the feotus nears the point where it could live outside the womb.

On June 24, 2022, the Supreme Court overturned Roe versus Wade, stating that there was no longer a federal constitutional right to an abortion. This ruling brought about the ethical dilemmas of the issue of the empowerment of women, their autonomy of self-determination versus the state's duty of care to protect the unborn child. Social workers supporting women in these circumstances will be faced with these dilemmas as described above.

5: Evaluation or review of care-plans.

This is very a useful process in social work hence it is important for social workers to have the ability to evaluate or review a care-plan as it gives them the opportunity to examine whether the stated aims or goals of the care-plan have been achieved or not and then to end the interventions of the aspects of the care-plan that have been on those that have not been achieved and to work out strategies to achieve these outstanding outcomes with mutual consent with the service-users especially those with capacity and for those without capacity for the social worker to liaise with the significant others involved in the care and support of the service-user in meeting the remaining outcomes that have not been achieved. The evaluation or review of a care plan should be time-specific, for example how many times the review is expected but this can change depending on changes of circumstances or if there is risk of harm to self or to others or the service user is at risk of abuse or neglect. The evaluation or review of a care-plan should be done in collaboration and negotiation with all the professionals involved in the provision of care and support to the service-use and this should be coordinated by the personal (Key Worker) who is the legal care-coordinator to meet the mutually agreed outcomes with the service-user. MIND (2018) suggests that a review should focus on the following:

1: Have the circumstances or needs of the service-user changed?

2: What is working in the plan?

3: Have the outcomes set out in the plan been achieved?

4: Are there new outcomes the service user wants to achieve?

5: Could improvements be done to achieve better outcomes?

6: Is the personal budget of the service-user appropriate and appropriately managed.

7: Are there changes to the service-users' network?

8: Is the service-use at risk of abuse or neglect?

9: Is the service-user and his or her carer, advocate satisfied with the care plan?

6: End of involvement, termination or closing a case.

This is the termination stage of the social work process after the objectives or outcomes of a care plan have been achieved or when there are no longer further interventions required in the care and support or treatment of a service-user. This stage of social work involves the issue of separation for both the service-user and the social worker because both may be affected by a painful separation and therefore both need to plan carefully to end the relationship successfully (Payne, 1997). Both social worker and service-user may therefore need to work to address issues of 'denial, negative feelings, sadness, and a feeling of release and having made progress' (Payne, 1997 p:150). This is very important because separation can evoke a variety of emotions which include: helplessness, fear, shock, loneliness, abandonment, and rejection (Trevithick, 2000). Closing a care-plan also involves the acknowledgement of the views of all the professionals that contributed to the care-plan of the service-user. It is advised that 'a good ending can allow the understanding, knowledge or wisdom gained to be reviewed and consolidated in ways that can be built on and used in the future' (Trevithick, 2000 p:108).

7: Working in organisations:

Social workers are usually based in organisations where they work hence it is advisable for them to have the appropriate skills, abilities and knowledge required to work in such settings. For example, social workers are expected to work within the remits of the policies of organisations for instance policies relating to collecting, processing and storing of information or even lone working, reporting of incidents, health and safety procedures, absence and sickness reporting to name a few. Social workers are usually found in various organisations such as hospitals, schools, prison settings, community mental health teams, children and family settings, courts and probation services, housing and homelessness organisations as well voluntary organisations and social services departments and each of these has specific philosophy and culture usually social workers are expected to undergo a process of assimilation in the philosophy and culture of where they work. Davies (2012) stresses that the main component of for success for a social worker in planning the care required for a service user is the availability of resources and means of accessing them within the organisation. It is sometimes very frustrating for social workers to be inhibited of the lack of funds or resources after a care-plan has been formulated for a service-user to meet his or her care and support needs. On occasions, social workers will formulate a care-plan for a service-user and management will advise the social worker to take the care-plan to the funding panel for approval for funding and at times this is rejected due to lack of funds. This tendency in organisations inhibits the autonomy of the social worker who is legally accountable for the care-plan he or she formulates.

8: Developing professional competencies.

It is an expectation for registered social workers to regularly enhance or update their competencies to meet the ongoing economic forces by training, studying, and reading regularly to underpin their social work practice to continue to be registrants of the social work register. It is also particularly important for registered social workers to be aware of legal and theoretical frameworks to underpin their practice and guide their practice. There are various theories that are used in social work, three of these include:

1: Person centred approach gives social worker an 'empirically tested way of being within a relationship which draws inspiration from a belief in the value of and wisdom of each person no matter what the current predicament may be' (Thorne, 1997 p:179)'

2: System theory is also useful for social workers as it encourages professionals to see the problems of service-users as a part of a whole and to realise that the whole is greater than the sums of it's parts and in order to understand these problems, professionals must study the transitional processes that occur between the components of the system and in order to notice emerging patterns and organised relationships between the parts (Dallas and Draper 2000, Minuchin, 1974).

3: Psychoanalysis: a knowledge of this is also good for the professional development of social workers as this helps them to understand the underlying philosophy that people move through deferent stages in which they confront internal conflicts and the way the conflicts are resolved determines their ability to learn, to get along with others and to cope with anxiety and stressful situations (Berk, 2003, Gross, 1992).

Social workers possess statutory powers that they use in performing their roles. This means their powers and authority are derived from statute (Carr and Brayne, 2003). It is therefore important for social workers to understand statutory laws to underpin their practice as well as to enhance the competencies. It is an advantage to know the difference between statutory law and common law. According to Carr and Brayne (2003) common law pertains to 'established, traditional law as defined by the courts and develop from precedents', while 'statute law is that law that has been passed by parliament' p: 57. For example, the Children Act 1989, 'sets out in detail how the courts, local authorities, and others are to deal with the care and welfare of the children' (Carr and Brayne, 2003 p:61).

It is also advisable to read the principles of justice to enhance your knowledge as a social worker especially for fighting for social justice and advocating for the Rights and Liberties of service users and their carers. Below is the history of the Magna Carta and the Boston Tea Party. The Magna Carta is one of the fundamental charters that underpins justice. It came about in 1215 after King John the first violated ancient laws and customs by which England was governed. His subjects especially the Barons subsequently revolted and forced him to sign the Magna Carta which listed the Rights and Liberties of his citizens. Aspects of the principles of the Magna Carta may not be relevant nowadays but the principles are still important in the British legal system. For example, no freeman should be imprisoned or stripped of his or her Rights without legal due process, justice should not be sold or bought or denied, the presumption of innocence, everyone should be equal under the rule of law, the freedom of the Church as well as swift justice and a free legal system accessible for all are the principles embedded in the Magna Carta. Subsequent documents about the Rights and Liberties of people have emerged as a consequence of the Magna Carta, for example the Human Rights Act 1998 which stresses the fundamental Rights and Freedoms which everyone is entitled to, the Commonwealth Charter which was signed by the late Queen Elizabeth the second expresses the commitments of member states of the Commonwealth to the development of free and democratic societies, the acknowledgement of civil societies in supporting the goals and values of the commonwealth centred on democracy, human rights and the rule of law. The Magna Carta was signed in Runnymede, a stone throw from where the author of this book is resident. In reading about the Magna Carta, the Author of this book realised that if citizens' rights are constantly under threat, there will be tendency for the citizens to rise and confront those who they feel are violating the rights as evidenced in the Boston Tea Party incident. The Boston Tea Party incident was an American political protest by the 'sons of liberty' in Boston Massachusetts on the 16[th of] December 1773. The protest was against the May 10th Tea Act of 1773 which allowed a British East India company to sell tea from China in the American Colonies without paying taxes except those imposed by the Townshend Act. The 'sons of liberty' were not happy about the Townshend Act hence they felt that their Rights were violated and the reacted by dumping 342 chests of tea imported by the British East India company into the Boston habour. The British reacted harshly, and the conflict escalated into the American Revolution and the Tea Party became an important incident in the history of America. This incident demonstrates that when citizens feel that their Rights are constantly being violated, there is always a likelihood of reiteration which has the potential to escalate even into a revolution. As a social worker, it is important to know about other countries' history in order to be well informed especially when trying to fight for social justice.

Reflection in and on practice can also help enhance the competency of social workers. Payne (2002 } maintains that reflection in social work is very important because it encourages social workers to experiment with alternative safe approaches which eventually become incorporated into their ways of thinking and practising. He argues that reflection takes place in the minds of social workers as they practise (reflection-in-practice) and afterwards as they think about their practice and try to understand the events they have experienced (reflection-on action). Singh (2001) also maintains that practitioners can achieve effective critical reflection by doing the following:

1: Setting time for supervision.

2: Finding someone (professional colleague, manager) to help clarify and challenge tacit assumptions of professional practice and

3: Fostering a sense of openness and safe environment where practitioners can bring controversial and personally challenging professional issues for discussions.

The first stage of the reflective process is often triggered by an awareness of uncomfortable feelings and thought which arise from a realisation that the knowledge and method one was applying in a situation were unable to explain what was happening in that particular and unique situation.

Another aspect of enhancing the competency of social workers is related to a commitment to challenge inequalities and avoid discriminating and oppressing service uses, their relative or colleagues in performing their roles as social workers. Social workers should always practise in an anti-discriminatory way by 'challenging unfairness or inequalities in how services are delivered' to service-user (Braye and Preston-shoot, 1995 p:107). On the other hand, social workers should be aware that 'based on egalitarian principle, the moral and ethical positions of anti-oppressive practice are those which ask social workers to both understand and engage with the harsh realities within which they work, and their clients live, and to seek to change strategies' (Dominelli, 2002, p:7).

CHAPTER FIVE

BOOK REVIEWS (LEARNING ACTIVITIES)

1: Learning activity: Reading an Article in the British Journal of Criminology (2004: 44, 34-54) titled: 'Joined-up services to tackle youth crime' by Ros Burnett and Catherine Appleton

This article reports findings of a case study of a Youth Offending Team (YOT) at Oxfordshire and it's partnership with other agencies looking at the realities of joined-up services at three levels: Core practice (recognised specialism), Specialist projects (assessments, case-managements) and Strategic management (Collective public service responsibilities). In this article, the set-up of the joined up Youth Offending Team at Oxfordshire was associated to an analogy of a 'fruit salad', an analogy the authors went on to illustrate by stating that each agency within the said setting 'took on more of the core tasks and also learnt a trick or two from each other, their professional identities were merged within the YOT- fruit cake mixture' but that notwithstanding 'staff found that being in the same office was advantageous and marveled at the ease with which they could simply ask each other questions' and even a 'Police Officer justified some swearing and other bad language as typical of the way she would normally address people well-known to her and therefore as symptomatic of being genuine with a young person who might otherwise be less trusting', however, 'although there is little question that these new practices have impinged on the nature and quality of face-to-face work with young people, the social work ethic is a tough nut to crack' and in concluding the authors stressed that notwithstanding the aforementioned impingements, the social work ethic survived the overhaul of the youth justice system. In the article 'multi-agency' was regarded as the coming together of various agencies to address a problem and 'inter-agency' was regarded as the 'fusion and melding of relations between agencies'. This article enhanced my insight into the youth justice system with special reference to joined-up services and the limitations of this philosophy.

2: Learning Activity: Reading, analysing, and writing comments about an article from the British Journal of Social Work 2010, volume 40, number 2, March p462-479) titled: 'No Recourse, No Support: State Policy and Practice towards South Asian Women Facing Domestic Violence in the UK' by Sundari Anitha.

The author of this article looks at the issue of domestic violence amongst women using a sample of 30 South Asian women who had no recourse to public funds and were experiencing domestic violence. The author explored the experiences of the sample group in accessing health, welfare and legal services. The authors highlighted legislations such as section 21 of the National Assistance Act 1948, The Housing Act 1996, and the Local Authorities' duty to support those that have no resource to public funds but are deemed to be 'destitute plus'.

In concluding the author maintains that the No Recourse to Public Fund 'stipulation represents a serious obstacle to accessing services for a vulnerable group of women as it undermines women's ability to leave abusive relationships, to recover from the abuse and to build a new life'.

This learning activity enhanced my knowledge with special reference to legislations of destitution and the National Assistance Act 1948. It also gave me insight into issues related to domestic violence and the dilemmas and difficulties faced by women being abused and at the same time have no recourse to public funds which they need to improve their life-chances.

3: Learning Activity: Reading, analysing, and writing up comments about an article from the British Journal of Social Work (2010, volume 40, number 3, April p696-713: titled: 'The Views of Children and Young People on Being Cared for by Independent Foster-Care Provider' by Julie Selwyn, Hilary Saunders and Elaine Farmer.

This is a study commissioned by the Independent Fostering Provider (IFP): Foster Care Associates 'to examine the progress and the outcomes of children in their care over a one-year period'. Questionnaires were used to solicit views of children. Ethical issues with reference to conducting the study were resolved and consents were sought from appropriate authorities and parents prior to administering the questionnaires.

The study concluded that: overall the children expressed positive comments about their placements, their carers as well as their Foster-Care Associates Social Workers.

52% of the children stated that they were happy with their schooling, some also responded that their foster families were 'loving' and that they were happy and proud 'for making it work' in their foster homes. This learning activity informed my social worker practice in issues related to fostering.

4: Learning Activity: Reading, analysing, and writing down comments about an article from the British Journal of Social Work (2010, June, volume 40 Number 4, p1081-1099) title: 'Social Work Admissions: Applicants with Criminal Convictions-The Challenge of Ethical Risk Assessment' by Peter Nelson and Malcolm Cowburn.

This paper looks at the admissions of applicants (ex-offenders) into social work training programmes and the implications with special reference to risk assessment and management within the framework of the General Social Care Council in terms of ethical issues related to socially including ex-offenders into training and issues of protecting the public especially those deemed vulnerable. This learning activity gave me insight into the three dimensions highlighted in the paper in terms of assessing risk posed by ex-offenders which were:(a) epistemological Dimension relating 'to how societies construct risk and risk assessments' (b)psychological dimension-relating to 'scientific methodologies' for identifying and accurately assessing risk associated to people with criminal offences, and (c) sociological approaches relating to 'identifying the functions that societal pre-occupation with risk fulfil in communities and societies'.

5: Learning Activity: Reading, analysing, and writing up comments about an article from the British Journal of Social Work (2010, volume 40, number 5, July p1503-1516) titled: 'The Deprivation of Liberty Safeguards and People with Dementia: Implications for Social Workers' by Sandra Dwyer.

This article illustrates the framework of deprivation of liberty safeguards related to service users with dementia by highlighting procedural ways of depriving the liberty of the group with reference to the Mental Capacity Act 2005 in terms of legibility, assessment, and 'best interest'. It also explores the roles of the 'managing authority' (Hospital/Care Home) and that of a 'supervisory body' (a Primary Care Trust of Local Authority) as well as those of Social Workers and Independent Mental Capacity Advocates. The article also made reference to the code of practice of the Mental Health Act 1983 and its relationship to Deprivation of Liberty Safeguards. This learning activity enhanced my knowledge of the procedural aspects of deprivation of Liberty Safeguards.

6: Learning activity: Reading and writing up analysis of an article from the British Journal of Social Work (2010, July, volume 40, number 5, p1419-1433) titled: 'Familial Homicide and Social Work' by Mark Drakeford and Ian Butler.

This article examines two cases (Marie Calwell's in January 1974 and Aaron Gilbert's in May 2005) related to familial homicide and draws on the Domestic Violence Crime and Victims Act 2004 to discuss the implications of the cases. The article highlights instances where convictions were made since the 'relatively new offence of familial homicide, introduced by the Domestic Violence Crime and Victims Act 2004' using the above cases of 'two women whose children died violently at the hands of their partners and the actions of those public agencies who were associated with the events surrounding the children's deaths' especially the role of social worker who were associated with the said cases. The author concludes that the 'women convicted for familial homicide' were 'presented as entirely culpable' were villainised' and 'not only does responsibility fell to them as mothers of the children who died but their fathers and stepfathers and other relatives escaped censorship while as in the Maria Colwell case,' there was a willingness to accept responsibility on the part of the welfare agencies and professionals involved in her case.

This learning activity helped me in acknowledging that sometimes responsibilities have to be accepted when failures occur in social work and perhaps by doing so, weaknesses or failures will be avoided, and social work practice will be enhanced through reflection.

7: Learning Activity: Reading, analysing details and writing up comments about an article from the British Journal of Social Work (2010, June, volume 40, number 4, p1211-1228) titled: 'Balancing Risk and Innovation to Improve Social Work Practice' by Louise Brown.

This article looks at issues of innovations and risks and the author examines the dilemmas of organisations balancing innovations and dealing with the risks associated with these and the experiences of individuals attempting to be innovative. The author draws on examples from the United Kingdom and Australia and highlights the issues that are involved in making innovations and the risks that are inevitably involved using social work as a framework. The author looks at: (a) the vulnerability of the service users receiving social work services, (b) the lack of incentives (c) the relevant legislations and (d) scarce resources which affect innovations and the risks that are involved within a social work context. The author uses the following examples: (a) 'family conferencing (UK) which the author describes as a bottom-up process innovation' which is related to 'making decisions about children who had been identified as in need or at risk' (b) Direct Payment which the author also described as a 'bottom-up' innovation, and (c) 'The New Parent Information Network (NEWPIN) imported from the UK to Australia that relates to the belief that creating a 'centre-based-in service in which parents could attend every day to tap into a programme of intensive education and support largely supported by peers and (d) 'The Intensive Family Based Service (IFBS) imported from the USA to Australia, an innovation that relates to 'adopting a strength-based approach' to provide in-home support to families in crisis where children are at point of removal. In concluding the author highlighted some of the interlinked risks associated with the above-mentioned innovations. Some highlighted included: rationing of resources versus increasing demand of services (poor use of resources), balancing service users' rights versus risks, and the uncertainty around sustainable funding.

This learning activity gave me insight into another area of social work I am not familiar with especially about innovations in Australia.

8: Learning activity: Reading, analysing, and writing up comments about an article from the British Journal of Social Work (2010, volume 40, number 3, April p772-788) titled: 'A Friend and Equal': Do young People in Care Seek the Impossible from their Social Workers?' Alison Mcleod.

This article looks at the relationship between social workers and young people in care and solicited the youngsters' views on the role of a social worker with reference to their experiences of being in care, whether they were consulted and involved in planning and how their grievances and complaints were dealt with. The author drew on the related literature and interviewed youngsters from the ages of nine to eighteen years. Ethical issues were resolved prior to conducting the study on all White youngsters but the author compensated for this by exploring the views of youngsters from other ethnicities within the literature reviewed.

From the study it was noted that the youngsters' answers 'indicated that they did not feel that their concerns were listened to and that 'they had limited confidence in the available channels for redress'. They also expressed views that 'the quality of care was often inadequate, and that they were marked out as different and troublemakers just because they were in public care'. Amongst other things, some youngsters regarded a good social worker as a professional who sorts things out, makes a difference. Other youngsters saw social workers 'as never doing anything'. The youngsters also regarded their relationships with social work staff as friendly.

This learning activity informed my social work practice in terms of the perceptions and the experiences of youngsters in care and their views of social work staff.

9: Learning activity: Reading, analysing, and writing up comments about an article from the British Journal of Social Work (2011, Volume 41, number 3, April, p539-556) titled: 'Religion in the Lives of unaccompanied minors: An Available and Compelling Coping Resource' by Muireann Ni Raghallaigh.

The author draws on the literatures as well as on 'interviews undertaken with unaccompanied minors living in the Republic of Ireland' to show how religious coping was a way for the above-mentioned minors in dealing with challenges they faced. The Author observed unaccompanied- minors living in a hostel and administered 'semi-structured-interviews'. In total eighteen females and fourteen males were interviewed. Consents were sought from the appropriate authorities for the study. The youngsters selected for the study were from Eastern Africa, Western Africa, Western Asia, Eastern Europe, and other parts of Africa. The study concluded that 'religious coping helped the young people to deal with the challenging circumstances with which they were faced' and religion provided them with meaning, comfort, and an increased sense of control in their new lives in the Republic of Ireland.

This learning activity made me to be more aware of the importance of religion to minors. It also made me to acknowledge the advice of the author that religion should not be imposed on service users rather service users should be allowed to self-determine their religion.

10: Learning Activity: Reading and analysing an article from the British Journal of Social Work (2011, volume 41, number 3, April p467-485) titled: 'The Pursuit of Integration in the Assessment of Older People with Health and Social Care Needs' by Michelle Abendstern, Jane Hughes, Paul Clarkson, Caroline Sutcliffe, and David Challis.

This article looks at the Single Assessment Process (SAP) and the quest to integrate assessments into a single assessment which can be used to meet the health and social needs of service users within the framework of government's guidance as well as the implications on other processes such as the Care Programme Approach and The NHS & Community Care Act 1990.

For the above study, data was examined, and respondents' views solicited at three levels: 'strategic', 'process' and 'practice' levels about the integration of assessments into one.

In concluding, the authors maintained that SAP was regarded as a core assessment data for accessing intermediate care and Care Management for people with long term conditions but rarely accepted for accessing health funded continuing care or mental health support. The authors also noted that 'Social Workers were the professional groups most frequently engaged in SAP regardless of setting, followed by District Nurses and Occupational Therapists.

The learning activity informed my social work practice in terms of single assessment. It also gave me awareness of the dilemmas of professionals in conducting SAP with varied professional training and skills.

11: Learning activity: Reading, analysing, and writing up comments about an article from the British Journal of Social Work (2009, volume 39, number 8, December p1615-1622) title: 'Adult Mental Health in a Changing International Context: The relevance to Social Work' by Shula Ramon.

This is a critical commentary by the author about the provision of mental health services and the changes that have impacted on these provisions. The author examines the role of Social Workers amid these trends as well as service users alongside the impact on the communities where people with mental ill health live. The author reviewed the relevant literatures and stated that the provision of mental health services has been moving in the direction of 'recovery' which entails' a shift from a deficit, chronic and hegemonic medicalised perspective of mental ill health' with increasing degree of service-user's control over his or her life. This learning activity informed my practice of social work around the relatively new area of the recovery model with special reference to mental health within an international context.

12: Learning activity: Reading and analysing an article from the British Journal of Social Work (2009, volume 39, number 6, September p1118-1137) titled: 'Working Girls: Abuse or Choice in Street-Level Sex Work? A study of Homeless Women in Nottingham' by Rachel Harding and Paul Hamilton.

In this research, twenty-six homeless women were interviewed by using structured, quantitative questionnaires in a case study-design from which information was collected about the relationship between a woman's experience of abuse and coercion and her decision to sex- work. From the literature-review, sex-work was referred to as the process of selling sex for money. The research was commissioned by a Charity for homeless people in Nottingham. Varied issues were explored in the research, some of these included victimhood, drug use, anti-social concerns and abuses perceived by the women involved in the research. Prior to conducting the research, ethical issues were given 'full consideration.' The findings of the research revealed that nine women who sex- worked claimed that they had done so because they 'needed the money either to pay for drugs and/or simply to alleviate the symptoms of poverty' while others indicated that there was more than one reason as to why they sex worked. The authors also identified various abuses experienced by the women interviewed which included domestic violence, emotional abuse, rape, sexual abuse, verbal abuse, neglect, financial abuse. Amongst the aforementioned, there was also 'the presence of coercion by the individuals significant to the women'.

The author also highlighted the role of social service and other agencies in dealing with the women who sex-worked. This leaning activity gave me insight into the traumatic experiences of women who sex-work.

13: Learning Activity: Reading, Analysing, and writing comments about an article from the British Journal of Social Work (2009, volume 39, number 6, September p1154-1174) titled: 'Growth in the Shadow of War: The Case of Social Workers and Nurses Working in a Shared War Reality' by Rachel Lev-Wiesel, Hadass Goldblatt, Zvi Eisikovits and Hanna Admi.

The article is about a study aimed to 'assess post-traumatic stress symptoms and Vicarious Traumatization (VT) versus post-traumatic growth (PTG) among Israeli practitioners who shared war- related reality with their clients during the Second Lebanon-Israeli War (2006)'. In the study, vicarious traumatization was described as a 'process by which the therapist's inner experience is negatively transformed through empathic engagement with the client's trauma material' and post- traumatic growth (PTG) was associated to ability to cope or of experiencing positive changes after the trauma in terms of personal strength, relationships with others.

The sample of the above study was selected two months after the aforementioned war and a sample of 204 practitioners (nurses, social workers, residents of the Haifa town in the above mentioned area were selected and questionnaires (self-reporting) were administered to them to gather information and to assess the extent to which positive or negative changes shared with their trauma-survivors clients affected them with special reference to traumatic events resulting from the aforementioned war or living under the shadow of war in general.

The study's findings were consistent with previous ones that maintain that practitioners who work with trauma survivors in a shared war reality may find the work to be stressful and even traumatic but also challenging and a source of personal growth. This learning activity was useful as it provided a source of reflection on my practice as I previously worked with a service-user with the above-mentioned cultural background.

14: Learning Activity: Reading, analysing, and writing up comments about an article from the British Journal of Social Work (2011, volume 41, number 1, January, p148-165) titled: 'Disabled Women, Domestic Violence and Social Care: The Risks of Isolation, Vulnerability and Neglect' by Gill Hague, Ravi Thiara and Audrey Mullender.

The article looks at the issues of disabled women experiencing domestic violence and the services available to them. The 'Big Lottery Fund' funded this research which was undertaken to look at the needs of abused, disabled women with physical and sensory impairments in the UK, the scope of existing provisions of services for the above service-user-group and to make recommendations. The said research was conducted between 2005 and 2008. A multi-method approach mainly qualitative in design was employed to conduct the research.

Some of the conclusion of the research indicated that disabled women experienced abuses from their carers who very often made use of the women's impairment. It was also found out that 'disabled women appeared to experience greater hurt and damage at the hands of abusers compared to non-disabled women' and that 'substantially less provision' of services were available to disabled abused women in comparison to non-disabled women. This learning activity helped to give me insight into issues related to disabled women.

15: Learning Activity: Reading, Analysing, and writing down comments about an article from the British Journal of Social Work (2011, volume 41, number 3, April p557-575) titled: 'Investing in the Future: Social Workers Talk about Research' by Liz Beddoe.

This article presents findings of a 'quantitative study of continuing professional education in New Zealand Social Work'. The study was conducted by interviewing social workers who were professional leaders, managers and employed in social work. The author regarded the selected sample group as having 'significant contemporary discourse of research –informed practice within the profession'. The views of the above sample were solicited about social work research, scholarship, and components of continuing social work education. It was concluded that Social Workers felt they were seen as less than robust intellectually. They were also conscious of their lack of confidence and prone to defending by reverting to practical conceptualisations of social work activity. In addition to this, it was observed by the authors that social workers largely lack the resources in terms of time, money, skills, and confidence to ensure their work is underpinned by scholarship and research. This learning activity throws light into the professionalization of social work in an international context, which is my orientation.

16: Learning Activity: Reading, analysing, and writing down comments about an article from the British Journal of Social Work (2011, volume 41, number 1, January, p131-147) titled: 'Social Work with Older People-Reducing Suicide Risk: A Critical Review of Practice and Prevention' by Jill Manthorpe and Steve Iliffe.

This article looks at suicide among older people using a theoretical framework in the face of complex body of evidence to construct practice-focused priorities with reference to examining suicide among older people. The lower limit of the age used in the research was sixty-five years. Reading this article did not really help me much as it failed to pin-point ways to prevent suicide amongst older people as the literature the authors reviewed for the research was not specific as indicated by their title, they dwelled too much on highlighting the lack of research related to suicide amongst older people.

17: Learning Activity: Reading, analysing, and writing down comments about an article from the British Journal of Social Work (2016, volume 46, number 2, March, p:339-354) titled: 'Reclaiming humanity: from capacities to capacities in understanding parenting in adversity' by Gupta, Anna et al.

This article explores the concept of Capacity Approach developed by Amartya Sen and examines how this concept can be employed in parenting and maltreatment.

Gupta et al (2016) outlined how the above approach can be used to inform professionals' understanding of the impact of policies on families living in poverty, especially those involved in the child protection system. In the literature review, poverty is regarded as a 'capacity deprivator' because of it's 'interference with the person's ability to make valued choices and participate fully in society'.

Using the capacity approach, they argued that there is both a moral and legal imperative to rethink child welfare policies related to families living in poverty. They suggested that Capacity Approach offers a 'framework for the development of more humane and socially just work practice'. They went on to suggest that Capacity Approach can be used to assess individuals' well-being, evaluate social arrangements, and develop policies and practices to effect social change. Gupta et al (2016) further highlighted that the core components of Capacity Approach consist of:

1: The resources available to a person – regarded as the 'means'.

2: Who the person is and what he or she does--regarded as 'functionings'

3: The person's social and environmental factors that inhibit the person's ability to transform means into functioning regarded as 'conversion factors'.

Gupta et al (2016) further highlighted that the differences in capacities to function can arise even with the same set of personal means for several reasons which can include:

1: Physical and mental heterogeneities e.g., disability or illness

2: Variation in 'non-personal' resources e.g., community resources

3: Environmental diversity e.g., threats of crime where someone is domiciled.

4: Differences in positions relative to others in the catchment area where someone is domiciled e.g., experiencing poverty while living in an affluent environment may transfer to absolute poverty in terms of the person's capacity.

5: Distribution of rules within the family may inhibit a personal's capacity within the family.

In concluding Gupta et al (2016) argued that policies increasing poverty and inequalities serve to reduce the means available to families hence conversion factors are reduced hence families' capacities are inhibited. However, they stressed that although more work is needed in the field of Capacity Approach, this notwithstanding, this approach offers a critical and ethical social work practice that promotes human dignity, and it incorporates a multidisciplinary assessment and analysis of factors that impact on people's lives with special reference to families and children in terms of enhancing their capacities.

This learning activity gave me insight into the concept of capacity approach with special reference to facilitating service-users' capacity for them to actualise their full potentials.

18: Learning Activity: Reading, analysing, and writing up comments about an article from the British Journal of Social Work (2016, Volume46, number1 January, P63-80) titled: 'Social Workers as Members of Community Mental Health Teams for older people: what is the added value?' by Abendstern, Michelle et al.

A study carried out by Abendstern et all (2017) by means of interviews and qualitative data collection drawn from a multiple case study of community mental health teams for older people, some with and others without social workers. The interviews consisted of questions about the teams' roles and the impact of the presence or absence of social workers on the teams' functioning. Abendstern et al (2017) employed a 'grounded theory approach' to analyse the data collected. Quantitative data collected and analysed were centred on individuals' role within the team and make-up of their caseloads, their views of other professionals within the team, the extent of role-blurring and their views on these. They also explored the history of the involvement of social workers in community mental health teams. They cited the work of Nolan (1993) that claimed that 'it was the closure of mental health hospitals from the 1960s and the consequent need to provide care and support in the community that precipitated the development of a new type of service in which the role of social workers was recognised as being crucial'. The above study found out that service-users' social care outcomes were significantly 'advanced' by the inclusion of social workers in the Community Mental Health Teams that participated in the study. It was also found out that the presence of both health and social care professionals was regarded to be good as the professionals complemented each other in terms of their skills and experiences as they possessed the ability to offer high quality care and support.

This learning activity adds to my existing experience as a Social Worker who has had several opportunities of working in Community Mental Health Teams and the role, we play in supporting Service Users.

19: Learning Activities: Reading, analysing, and writing up about an article from the Institute of Development-Studies-Bulletin (2012) Volume 43 number 4 July p49-72 titled 'A Force for Good'? Police Reform in Post-Conflict Sierra Leone by Charley, Chris P Joseph and M'Cormack, Ibiduni

Charley and M'Cormack (2012) traced the history of the Sierra Leone Police Force to the British Colonial administration, narrated it to post-independent days and up to the outbreak of the civil conflict in 1991 which largely 'decimated the force' and they went on to ask the question whether a police reform is a force for good in post-conflict Sierra Leone. Charley and M'Cormack (2012) started their narrative by looking at the origin of the Sierra Leone Police Force from the time of the West Africa Frontier Force which was responsible for maintaining Britain's colonial frontier as well as maintaining law and order in the aforesaid region between 1863 and 1906. They went on to state that from 1906, the police force in the aforesaid region was 'modelled after the British police force and became part of the civic service'. They further stated that the Sierra Leone Police force was 'considered one of the best and well-disciplined forces in British West Africa' and it was twice commended by the Royal Commission for 'it's excellent handling of civil disturbances in Freetown and the provinces' between 1955-56. The role of the Sierra Leone Police force started to change from 1964 with the passing of an Act in Parliament as well as consolidating and amending the Law that related to the 'organisation, discipline, power and duties of the police' alongside the setting up of a police council with the minister of the interior as chairman. The above-mentioned Act defined the role of the Sierra Leone Police Force with special reference to 'the detection of crime and the apprehension of offenders of law and order, the protection of life and property and the enforcement of all laws and regulations with which they are directed' as per Act number 4 of the Sierra Leone Police Act 1964. The Sierra Leone Police Force's role took another dimension after independence and during the one-party system. During the aforementioned period, the then President made the Commissioner of Police a member of the ruling party and a nominated member of parliament and a cabinet minister, maintained Charley and M'Cormack (2012). At the same time, the 'nomenclature' of Commissioner of Police was changed to 'Inspection General of Police' and these changes impacted on the execution of the role of the Sierra Leone Police Force with special reference to the morale and discipline of the said force, asserted Charley and M'Cormack (2012). In a move to consolidate democracy in Sierra Leone in 1996, several advisory councils were setup, one of these was an Advisory Council formed that was geared towards looking at the challenges of the Sierra Leone Police Force and this was headed by the then president who was a lawyer by profession. The Advisory Council that was set up recommended amongst other things the following:

1: The restoration of the friendly image of the Sierra Leone police force and the maintaining of good community relations.
2: The establishment of a planning unit to project police training and to look at the equipment needs of the police force
3: The decentralisation of the Sierra Leone Police Force with an Inspector General, a Deputy Inspector General and a Senior Commissioner of Police at the headquarters in Freetown and officers at each provisional level and at divisional head quarters
4: Reducing the Sierra Leone Police force as well as working towards enhancing the quality of intake of capable university educated men and women by ensuring that the point of admission is equivalent to Cadet status.
5: Providing the Sierra Leone Police force with adequate equipment and emoluments to enable members of the force to perform their duties effectively and to motivate them respectively. When the Chairman of the Advisory Council subsequently became the president of Sierra Leone in 1996, he ensured that the above cited recommendations were pursued by consolidating and establishing the Sierra Leone Police Council under the chairmanship of the Vice President at the time. The Police Council subsequently developed a working document of Policing Ethics, a process of professionalisation that was enhanced by the support of the UK Department for International

Development (DFID), the UNDP and other agencies. However, the journey to reforming the Sierra Leone Police was diverted when a coup d'etat took place in Sierra Leone on 25th May 1997 perpetrated by elements of the Sierra Leone Army which subsequently joined up with the RUF to form the Armed Forces Revolutionary Council regime, this led to many senior Police Officers to flee Sierra Leone reported Charley and M'Cormack (2012). In combating the unrest in Sierra Leone, the Economic Community of West African States Monitoring Group (ECOMOG) arrived in Sierra Leone and helped to drive the Rebels from Freetown and the President returned to power in 1998 and he continued with the Police reforms and in doing so, a request was made to the Commonwealth and the United Nations. Consequently, two International Police teams arrived in Sierra Leone under the 'auspices of the Commonwealth Police Development Taskforce (CPDTF) and the United Nations Observer Mission in Sierra Leone (UNOMSIL)', stated Charley and M'Cormack (2012). The above-mentioned teams sought to work out a policing model best suitable for Sierra Leone. As most of the above team-members were from the Commonwealth, they had 'one significant area of policing in common-the tradition of common law, rather than civil law systems', reported Charley and M'Cormack (2012). Another transformation that occurred was the introduction of the Sierra Leone Police Charter in August 1998 that was geared towards the 'primacy on the police as providers of internal security in Sierra Leone' highlighted Charley and M'Cormack (2012). The overall aim of the Charter was 'to see a reborn Sierra Leone Police, which will be a force for good' cited Charley and M'Cormack (2012).

However, the authors of this article were a little bit ambivalent with reference to whether reforming the police force in post conflict Sierra Leone was a force for good, an ambivalence probably brought about by inhibitors such as corruption and the politicking of the Police Force as well as the scarce resources needed to carry the reforms through. However, it appeared the reforms enhanced the professionalisation of the Sierra Leone Police for example the establishment of the complaint, Discipline and internal investigation department, the establishment of internal audit department as well as that of the corporate service department and the equal opportunity department as well as the establishment of the Family Support Unit Department (FSU) responsible for responding to cases related to sexual and gender-based violence, arms of processes of professionalisation. One of the ethical difficulties in policing in Sierra Leone is centred on enforcing the rule of law versus policing activities that are deemed to be deeply rooted in Sierra-Leone's tradition. One example of this was cited in this article involving a seven-year-old girl's mother who went to the police and reported that her daughter had been abducted and taken to be initiated in the Bondo society (regarded as female's rite of passage for girls), a custom that has lasted for years. The above incident was resolved by the Police by liaising with the traditional hierarchies in the catchment area of the incident by initially going to the Paramount Chief and narrating the details of the incident of abduction to him who summoned the 'Chief-Sowie' (female traditional head of the Bondo Society) to hear from her what she knew about the abducted girl. Consequently, it was agreed to discuss the incident with the Chief Medical Officer in preparation for meeting the medical needs of the girl. The

Medical Officer referred the case to a female chief-ward-sister, (a member of the Bondo society as well) who asked some female nurses who were also members of the Bondo society to participate in resolving the problem. Finally, the nurses and some female police officers (also members of the Bondo society) went into the setting where the girl was held and rescued her and provided her with medical care. This learning activity gave me an insight into the history of the Sierra Police Force and the reforms the force has undergone in the process of professionalisation. The article also informed me about the usefulness of multi-agencies working together towards achieving the same objectives, a component of Social Work. This article also gave me an awareness of the difficulties the Sierra Leone Police Force faces in terms of dealing with civil incidents that are deeply rooted in tradition.

1. Abendstern, M et al (2011)	The pursuit of integration in The assessment of older People with health and social Needs The British Journal of Social Work Volume 41, number 3, April, p.467-485
2. Abendstern M, Tucker S, Wilberforce M, Jasper R, Brand, C and Challis D (2016)	Social workers as members of community mental health teams for older people: what is the added value? The British Journal of Social Work Volume 46, number 1, January p.63-80
3. Agnew, T (2002)	The workplace stress epidemic [Internet], Available from: http://www.channel4.com/health/microsites/0-9/4health/stress/saw-work.html [Accessed 5th February 2005]
4. Allen, R (ed) (2002)	The Penguin Dictionary London, Penguin
5. American Psychiatrist Association (1994)	Diagnostic Statistical Manual Mental Disorders 4th edition Washington, American Psychiatric Association

6. Andrews, B and Brown, G (1995)	Stability and change in low self-esteem, the role of psychosocial factors Psychological Medicine, Volume 25, p23-31
7. Angold, E. J et al (1998)	Puberty and depression: the role of age, puberty and pubertal timing Psychological Medicine, volume 28, p.51-61
8. Anitha, S (2010)	No recourse, no support: state policy and practice towards South Asian Women facing Domestic violence in the UK The British Journal of Social Work Volume 40, number 2, March p.462-479
9. Atkinson, R et al (2000)	Hilgard's introduction to psychology 13th edition, Orlando, Harcourt College
10. Ballock, J et al (1998)	Working in the social services: Job satisfaction, stress and Violence, British Journal, volume 28, p.329-350
11. Ballock, J et al (eds) (2003)	Social Policy 2nd edition Oxford, Oxford University Press
12. Barn, R (2000)	Black youth on the margins A research review Joseph Rowntree Foundation
13. Beddoe, L (2011)	Investing in the future: social workers talk about research The British Journal of Social Work Volume 41, number 3, April p.557-575

14. Bee, H (2000)	The developing child, 9th edition Needham Heights, Allyn and Bacon
15. Benner, P (1984)	Stress and satisfaction in the Job: Work meanings and coping of mid-career men New York, Praeger
16. Berk, L (2003)	Development through the lifespan 3rd edition Boston, Allyn and Baron
17. Birch, T and Malim (1998)	Introductory Psychology London, Macmillan Press Ltd
18. Booth, A B (1985)	Stressmanship London, Savern House
19. Bradley, J and Sutherland, V (1995)	Occupational stress in social work A comparison of social workers and home-care staff British Journal of Social Work Volume 25, 1995, p313-331
20. Brent, D and Birmaher, B (2002)	Adolescent depression [Internet], Available from: http://www.medical-journals.com1ahm [Accessed 11 April 2004]
21. The British Association of Social Workers (2003)	Code of ethics for social work [Internet], Available from: http://www.basw.co.uk [Accessed 21 October 2003]
22. British Medical Association (2003)	Adolescent Health London, British Medical Association
23. Brown, EL. L (1942)	Social work as a profession New York, Russell Foundation
24. Brown, G and Harris, T (1978)	Social origins of depression A study of psychiatric Disorder in women London, Tavistock publication

25. Brown, L (2010)	Balancing risk and innovation to improve social work practice <u>British Journal of social work</u> Volume 40, number 4, June, p.1211-1228
26. Buglass, D (1996)	<u>A workforce in transition, the careers and experiences of the staff of the social work department</u> [Internet] Available from: <u>http://www.scotland.gov.uk/cru/ documents/rs23-01.htm</u> [Accessed 26th January 2005]
27. BUPA (2004)	Stress in the workplace [Internet] Available from: <u>http://hcd2.bupa.co.uk/fact-sheets/ htm/stress-workplace.html</u> [Accessed 5th March 2005]
28. Burnett, R and Appleton, C (2004)	Joined-up service to tackle youth Crime <u>The British Journal of Criminology</u> 44, number 3, 2004, p34-54
29.Bushy, A et al (2004)	<u>The effects of a stress management Program on knowledge and perceived self-efficiency among participants from a faith community: a pilot study</u> [Internet], Available from: < <u>http://www.rno.org/journal/issues/ vol-4/issues2/Bushy-article.htm</u>> [Accessed 3rd May 2005]
30. Career Resource Centre (2005)	<u>A job satisfaction measure</u> [Internet], Accessed from: <u>http://www.career-resource.net/jobtest.php</u> [Accessed 28th January 2005]

31. Charley, C. P. J and M'Cormack, F. I (2012)	A force for good? Police reform in post conflict Sierra Leone <u>Institute of Development studies Bulletin</u> Volume 43, number 4, July, p.49-72
32. Chartered Institute of Personnel and development (2003)	<u>Stress, health, safety and wellbeing</u> [Internet], Available from: <u>http://www.cipd.co.uk/subjects/ health/stress.htm</u> [Accessed, 4th May 2005]
33. Coffey, M et al (2004)	Stress in social services: mental wellbeing, constraints and job satisfaction <u>The British Journal of social work</u> Volume 34, number 5, July 2004, p735-746
34. Coleman, J and Roker, D (eds) (2001)	<u>Supporting parents of teenagers</u> <u>A handbook for professionals</u> London, Jessica Kingsley
35. Cooper, C. L and Earnshaw, J (2001)	<u>Stress and employer liability</u> <u>2nd edition</u> London, Chartered Institute of Personnel Development
36. Cooper, C. L, Sloan, S J and Williams, S, S (1998)	<u>Occupational stress indicator</u> Windsor, NFER-Nelson
37. Cox, T et al (2000)	<u>Research on work-related stress</u> <u>Report to the European Agency</u> <u>For safety and health at work</u> [Internet], Accessed from : <u>http://agency.osha.ed.int/ publicaions/reports/stress.htm</u> [Accessed 26th January 2005]
38. Cox, T and Rial-Gonzalez (2004)	<u>Work-related Stress: the European</u> <u>Picture</u> [Internet], Accessed from: <u>http://agency.osha.eu.int/publications/ magazine/5en/index-3.htm</u> [Accessed]26th January 2005]

39. Currie, C and Todd, J (2003)	Mental wellbeing among school Children in Scotland: age and cross national comparison Edinburgh, HBSC
40. David, P (1998)	Stress in Social Work London, Jessica Kingsley
41. Department of health (2003)	Promoting the status of social work A consultation on the timetable to implement protection of the title of 'Social Worker' London, Department of Health
42. Dominelli, L (1997)	Sociology for social workers Basingstoke, Palgrave
43. Douglas, A and Philpot, T (1998)	Caring and coping, a guide to social services London, Routledge
44. Drakeford, M and Butler, I (2010)	Familial homicide and social work The British Journal of Social Work Volume 40, number 5, July 2010, p1419-1433
45 Dwyer, S (2010)	The deprivation of liberty safeguards and people with dementia implication for social workers The British Journal of Social Work Volume 40, number 5 July 2010, p.1503-1516
46. Engineering Employers Federation (2001)	Managing stress at work London, Engineering Employers Federation
47. Fergusson, D M et al (2000)	Risk factors and life process associated with the onset of suicidal behaviour during adolescence and early adulthood Psychological Medicine Volume 30, issue 1 January 2000 p.23-39

48. Freidson, E (1994)	Professionalism Reborn Theory, prophesy and policy Cambridge, Polity Press
49. Froneberg, B (2003)	Psychological stress and wellbeing at work African newsletter on occupational Health and safety Volume 13, August 2003 p32-34
50. Fox, K (1997)	Mirror, Mirror A summary of research findings On body image [Internet], Accessed from: http://www.sic.org/public/mirror.htl [Accessed 24 February 2004]
51. Gangster, D et al (1986)	The role of social support in the experience of stress at work Journal of Applied Psychology Volume 71, issue 1 March 1986 p.102-110
52. General Social Care Council (2002)	Code of practice for social workers And code of practice for employers of social workers London, General Social Care Council
53. Ghuman, P S (1996)	Asian Adolescents in the West Leicester, The British Psychological society
54. Goldberg, D et al (1997)	The validity of two versions of the GHQ in the WHO study of mental illness in General Health care Psychological Medicine Volume 27, issue 1, January 1997 p.191-197

55. Goodyer, M et al (1993)	Depression in 11-16-year-old Girls: the role of past parental psychopathology and exposure to recent life events <u>Journal of Child and psychiatry and allied disciplines</u> Volume 34, number 7, November 1993 p.1103-1115
56. Graham, A (1990)	<u>Teach yourself statistics 2nd edition</u> Oxon, Bookpoint
57. Gray, P (2002)	<u>Mental Health in the workplace</u> <u>Tackling the effects of Stress</u> [Internet], Accessed from: http://www.org/st.com./reseach/22htm [Accessed, 15th January 2005]
58. Gross, R D (1992)	<u>Psychology, the science of mind and behaviour</u> London, Hodder and Stoughton
59. Gross, R D and McIlveen, R (1998)	<u>Psychology a new introduction</u> Kent, Hodder & Stoughton
60. Gupta, A et al (2016)	Reclaiming humanity: from capacities to capacities in understanding parenting in adversity <u>The British Journal of Social work</u> Volume 46, number 2, March 2016 p.339-354
61. Hampshire County Council (1997)	Managing work-related stress Report of Director of social services [Internet], Accessed from: http://www.hants.gov.uk/scmxn/c23215.html [Accessed, 23rd January 2005]

62. Harding, R and Hamilton, P (2009)	Working girls: abuse or choice In street-level sex work? A study of homeless women in Nottingham <u>British Journal of Social Work</u> Volume 39, number 6 September 2009 p.1154-1174
63. Harper, W M (1991)	<u>Statistics 6th edition</u> London, Longman Group UK Ltd
64. Hague, G et al (2011)	Disabled women, domestic violence and social care: the risk of isolation, vulnerability and neglect <u>The British Journal of Social Work</u> Volume 41, number 1 January 2011 p.148-165
65. Health and Safety Executive (2001)	<u>Work-related Stress, a short Guide</u> London, Health and Safety Executive
66. Health and Safety Executive (2005)	<u>Work-related Stress</u> [Internet], Accessed from: <u>http://www.sh.gov.uk/lan/lacs/81-4.htm</u> [Accessed 4th May 2005]
67. HM Prison & Probation, Ministry of Justice (2020)	<u>Mentally Disordered Offenders-the</u> <u>restricted patient system</u> [Internet], Accessed from: http:gov.uk/government/pulications/ mentally-disordered-offenders-the restricted-patient-#publications-update history [Accessed 26TH December 2022]
68. Hilpern, K (2002)	<u>Social Work; Many more returns</u> [Internet], Accessed from: <u>http://www.jobsindependent.co.ukhtm</u> [Accessed 23rd April 2005]
69. Holden, R (1992)	<u>Stress Busters 101 ways to inner calm</u> London, Thorsons
70. Horwath, J and Morrison, T (1999)	<u>Effective training in social care</u> <u>From theory to practice</u> New York, Routledge

71. Houston, S (2010)	Beyond Homo Economicus: Recognition, Self-realization and Social Work The British Journal of Social Work Volume 40 number 3, April 2010 P.841-857
72. Hutman, S et al (2005)	Stress management at work and at home [Internet], Accessed from: http://www.helpguide.org/mental/stress-management-relief-coping.htm [Accessed 3rd May 2005]
73. International Labour Organisation (2000)	Safework: developing a workforce stress prevention programme [Internet], Accessed from: http://www.ilo.org/public/english/protection/safework/stress/prevggm.htm
74. Jackson, J A (ed) (1970)	Professions and Professionalisation London, Cambridge University Press
75. Johnson T J (1972)	Professions and Power Basingstoke, Macmillan Press
76. Kadushin, A (1992)	Supervision in social work 3rd edition New York, University Press
77. Keith, C (2000)	A psychometric evaluation of occupational stress indicator [Internet], Accessed from: http://www.highbeam.com/library/doc1.asp [Accessed 28th January 2005]
78. Kenworth, N et al	Common Foundation studies in nursing London, Churchill Livingstone
79. Kinder, A (2004)	Stress audits: what are they and why bother [Internet], Accessed from: http://www.counsellingatwork.org.uk/journal-htm [Accessed 15th May 2005]

80. Kortum, E and Ertel, M (2003)	Occupational Stress and wellbeing at work-an overview of our current understanding and future directions _African newsletter on occupational health and safety_ Volume 13, August 2003, pp.35-38
81. Kutek, A (1998)	No Health, no service In David, R (1998) _Stress in Social Work_ London, Jessica Kingsley
82. Larson, L M (1995)	_The rise to professionalism_ _A sociological analysis_ Berkeley, University of California Press ltd
83. Lazarus, R S (1999)	_Stress and Emotion_ _A new synthesis_ New York, Springer
84. Leighton, P (1997)	_The work-environment_ _The law of health, safety_ _And welfare new edition_ London, Nicholas Brealey Publishers
85. Lev-Wiesel, R et al (2009)	Growth in the shadow of war: the case of social workers and nurses working in a shared war reality _British Journal of Social Work_ Volume 39, September 2009 pp.1154-1174
86. Levi, L (2000)	_Guidance on work-related stress_ _Spice of life or kiss of death_ Luxembourg, European Commission
87. London Hazard Centre (1996)	_Stress at Work_ London, London Hazard Centre
88. Lu, L et al (1999)	Perceived Work Stress and locus of control: a combined quantitative and qualitative approach _Research and Practice in Human Resource Management_ Volume 7, issue 1

89. Lundstrom, T et al (2002)	Organisational and Environmental Factors that affect worker health and safety and patient outcomes <u>American Journal of Infection Control</u> Volume 30, issue 2, April 2002 pp.93-106
90. Lymbery, M (1997)	Social Work at the crossroads <u>British Journal of Social Work</u> Volume 31, number 3, June 2001 pp.369-381
91. Macdonald, K.M (1995)	<u>The sociology of Professions</u> London, Sage Publications Ltd
92. Manthorpe, J and LLiffe, S (2011)	Social work with older people Reducing suicide risks: A critical review of practice and prevention <u>British Journal of Social Work</u> Volume 41, number 1, January 2011 pp.131-147
93. Martinez, C (2004)	<u>Job Stress and Job satisfaction in child Welfare: an analysis of the impact of group supervision</u> [Internet] Accessed from; <u>http://www.envisionjournal.com/ application/Article/htm</u> [Accessed 17th May 2005]
94. Mattiasson, I et al (1990)	Threat of unemployment and Cardiovascular risk factors: longitudinal study of sleep and serum cholesterol concentration in men threatened <u>British Medical Journal</u> Volume 301, September 1990 pp.461-466

95. McLaughlin K (2001)	Stress Vulnerability [Internet], Available from: http://www.spiked-online. com/2001/11/29stressing-vulnerabilityhtm [Accessed 25th June 2019]
96. Mcleod, A (2010)	'A friend and an equal': do young people In Care seek the impossible from their social workers? British Journal of Social Work Volume 40, number 3, 2010, April pp772-788
97. Metcalfe, C et al (2003)	A contemporary validation of the Reeder Stress inventory British Journal of Health Psychology Volume 8, issue 1, 2003, pp83-94
98. Meyer, C (1970)	Social Work Practice a Response to the urban crisis London, Collier-Macmillan Ltd
99. Michie, S and Williams, S (2002)	Reducing psychological work-related psychological ill health and sickness: a systematic literature review London, University of London
100. Mohajeri-Nelson, N (1999)	Stress level and job satisfaction: does a causal relationship exist? [Internet], Accessed from: http://www.webclearinghouse.net/volume/htm [Accessed 26th June 2019]
101. Montazeri, C (2003)	The 12-item general health questionnaire (GHQ-12) translation and validation study on the Iranian version Health Quality Life Outcomes Volume 1, number 1, 2003 p.1
102. Muirean, N (2011)	Religion in the lives of unaccompanied Minors: An available and compelling coping resource British journal of Social Work Volume 41, number 3 April 2011 pp.539-556

103. Murray, R (2005)	<u>Managing your stress</u> London, Royal College of Nursing
104. Nelson, P and Cowburn, M (2010)	Social Work admissions: applicants with criminal convictions-the challenge of ethical risk assessment <u>British Journal of Social Work</u> Volume 40, number 4, June 2010 pp.1081-1099
105. Neufeld, S (2005)	Work-related Stress: what you need To know [Internet], Accessed from: <u>http://healthyplace.healthology.</u> <u>com/printer-friendly..</u> [Accessed 3rd May 2005]
106. Nolen-Hoeksema, S et al (2003)	<u>Introduction to Psychology 14th edition</u> London, Thomson Learning
107. Nolen-Hoeksema, S and Girgus, S (1994)	The emergence of gender differences in depression during adolescence <u>Psychological Bulletin</u> Volume 115, number 3, May 1994, pp424-443
108. Palsson, M B et al (1991)	Burnout, empathy, and sense Of coherence among Swedish district nurses before and after systematic clinical supervision <u>Scandinavian Journal of Caring Sciences</u> Volume 10, number 1, 1991, pp19-26
109. Ostroff, C (1992)	The relationship between satisfaction, altitudes and performance: An organisational Level analysis <u>Journal of Applied Psychology</u> Volume77, number 6, December 1992, pp963-974
110. Onyett, S et al (1997)	Job satisfaction and burnout among Community mental health teams <u>Journal of Mental Health</u> Volume 6, Issue 1, 1997

111. Payne, R (1979)	Demands, Support, Constraints and Psychological health In Mackay, C and Cox, T (eds) <u>Response to stress: Occupational aspects</u> London, IPC Business Press
112. Penna, S et al (1995)	<u>Job Satisfaction and Dissatisfaction Amongst residential care workers</u> [Internet], Accessed from: <u>http://www.jrf.org.uk/knowledge/</u> <u>findingd/socialcare/SC.asp.htm</u> [Accessed 23rd April 2005]
113. Powel, T (1992)	<u>The Mental Health Handbook</u> Oxon, Winslow Press
114. Ramon, S (2009)	Adult Mental Health in changing international Context: the relevance to social work <u>British Journal of Social Work</u> Volume 39, number 8, December 2009, pp1615-1622
115. Reid et al (1999)	Explanations for stress and job Satisfaction in mental health professionals: a qualitative study <u>Social Psychiatry and Psychiatric epidemiology</u> Volume 34, Issue6, June 1999, pp301-308
116. Reuschemeyer, D, (1986)	<u>Power and Division of Labour</u> Oxford, Polity Press
117. Sassoon, M and Lindow, V (1995)	Consulting and empowering Black Mental Health Users In Fernando, S <u>Mental Health in a multi-ethnic</u> <u>Society</u> London, Routledge
118. Schafer, J and Fals-Stewart, W (1991)	Issues of method, design, and analysis procedure in psychological Research on stress <u>British Journal of Medical psychology</u> Volume 64, issue 4 December, pp375-382

119. Seed, P (1973)	Expansion of Social Work in Britain London, Routledge, and Kegan Paul ltd
120. Selwyn, J et al (2010)	The views of children and young people on being cared for by an independent Foster-Care Provider British Journal of Social Work Volume 40, number 3, April pp.696- 713
121. Smith, J (1997)	Stress at work-99 [Internet], Accessed from: http://www.isma.org.uk/stress/stresswork99.htm [Accessed: 26th January 2005]
122. Spector, P E (1997)	Job satisfaction, application, assessment, cause and consequence California, Sage Publication
123. Steinberg, L (1993)	Adolescence 3rd edition London, McGraw-Hill, inc.
124. Sutton, J (2000)	Thrive on stress: Managing Pressure and positivity thrive on it 2nd edition Oxford, How To Books
125. Sweeting, H and West, P (2002)	The Health of young people In Scotland: Quantitative dimension Glasgow, HEBS
126. Thomas, J and Daubman, K A (2001)	The relationship between friendships Quality and Self-Esteem in adolescent Girls and boys Sex Roles: A Journal of Research Volume 13, Issue 1-2, July 2001, p. 53-65
127. Thomson, L et al (2003)	Best Practice in rehabilitating Employers following absence due to work-related stress [Internet], Accessed from: http://www.hsegove.uk/research/r..htm [Accessed: 30th May 2005]
128. Williams, S et al (1998)	Improving the mental health of the NHS Trust Workforce London, Nuffield NHS Trust

129. Williams S, (1994)	Managing pressure for peak Performance : the positive approach to stress London, Kogan Page
130. Wilt, A (1992)	Professions and Patriarchy London, Routledge

Ingram Content Group UK Ltd.
Milton Keynes UK
UKHW051244180423
420361UK00012B/789